The Principles of Life in the Spirit

The Principles of Life in the Spirit

Romans 8

Paul Brewster

SUNESIS MINISTRIES LTD

The Principles of Life in the Spirit

Copyright © 2016 Paul Brewster. The right of Paul Brewster to be identified as author of this work has been asserted by him in accordance with the Copyright, Designs, and Patents Act 1988. All rights reserved. No part of this publication may be reproduced or transmitted in any form or by any means, electronic or mechanical, including photocopy, recording, or any information storage and retrieval system, without permission in writing from the author.

ISBN 978-0-9935147-6-0

Published by Sunesis Ministries Ltd. For more information about Sunesis Ministries Ltd, please visit:

www.stuartpattico.com

Unless otherwise indicated, Bible quotations are from the Holy Bible, King James Version.

Where indicated: Scripture quotations taken from the Amplified Bible, Copyright © 1954, 1958, 1962, 1964, 1965, 1987 by The Lockman Foundation. Used by permission. (www.Lockman.org)

The author of this book does not dispense medical advice or prescribe the use of any technique as a form of treatment for physical, emotional, or medical problems without the advice of a physician, either directly or indirectly. The intent of the author is only to offer information of a general nature to help you in your quest for emotional and spiritual well-being. In the event you use any of the information in this book for yourself, the author and publisher assume no responsibility for your actions.

The views expressed in this book are solely those of the author and do not necessarily reflect the views of the publisher, and the publisher hereby disclaims any responsibility for them.

I dedicate this book to Pastor Gary Bryden and Pastor Lorita Bryden who have been a great spiritual help support and example from the time I have known them.

My beautiful wife Lorraine Brewster, who has been a tremendous help to me during our 11 years marriage. My sweetheart.

Contents

Introduction	9
The Christian Identity in Christ	12
The Law of Works Versus the Righteousness of Faith	20
Having the Mind of the Spirit	27
Life in the Spirit	34
The Impact of the Divine Life in the Human Body	40
Living by the Spirit	49
The Spirit of Adoption	57
The Significance of Being the Children of God	66
The Manifestation of the Sons of God	76
The Firstfruits of the Spirit	83
Saved by Hope	91
Holy Spirit Intercession	98
God's Eternal Purpose for the Believer Part 1	106
God's Eternal Purpose for the Believer Part 2	116
The All-Sufficiency of Christ	127
How to be Victorious Over the Condemnation of the Devil	137
The Eternal Security of the Saints	147
Bibliography	157

Introduction

Living in the Western world, society has gravitated towards humanism and dependence on human intellect at the expense of true Christian spirituality. This ideology, with regret, is pervading the Church of Jesus Christ, consequently causing the divine power in God's people to wane and to be replaced by dependency on reasoning and the strategic mechanisms of philosophy and human wisdom which are frail, weak and therefore incapable of solving the varied societal problems of this present age.

I am reminded of the words of the Apostle Paul who uttered two of the signs that we were living in the last days saying,

"Having a form of godliness, but denying the power thereof...Ever learning and never able to come to the knowledge of the truth" (2 Tim. 3:5, 7).

Christendom exhibits an outward form of godly piety while not having the power to live and walk as Christ and His disciples walked. And with a great emphasis on education and learning in secular academic and Christian theology, many lives are not being changed because they are unable to come to the knowledge [Gk epignosis: experiential and intimate knowledge] of the truth. The reason is that many in Christendom have forsaken and neglected the ministry of the Holy Spirit: His wisdom, life and power and have settled for the deadness and inability of human wisdom and effort. Paul exhorts us that our faith should not stand in the wisdom of men but in the power of God which is the demonstration of the Spirit and power (1 Cor. 2:4-5). The wisdom of men is powerless, but the wisdom of God is dynamic and living, wrought by the Spirit (1 Cor. 1:24-25).

The divine agent of God's wisdom and power is the Holy Spirit, and it is our responsibility to depend on Him for guidance, direction and empowerment. The Christian's calling is to live the supernatural life rather than to live in your own self effort, struggling through life. Life in the Spirit was not designed to be a struggle but a rest. In the Spirit, you are empowered to live out your true identity in Christ and fulfil your destiny through the power of the Holy Spirit.

The purpose of my book is to teach and impart to you the principles and truths of living life in the Spirit so that you can unlock God's supernatural ability in you which will cause you to exceed your own natural capability and those of your peers in every walk of your calling in life. Paul's prayer, recorded in Scripture, was for every believer to be given the spirit of wisdom and revelation (Eph. 1:17); to what end:

"That the God of our Lord Jesus Christ, the Father of glory, may give unto you the spirit of wisdom and revelation in the knowledge of him: The eyes of your understanding being enlightened; that ye may know what is...the exceeding greatness of his power to us-ward who believe, according to the working of his mighty power" (Eph. 1:17-18a, 19+).

The spirit of wisdom and revelation is to help us to see what belongs to us and walk into it. You cannot walk in what God has promised until you first see it, because what you see is what you become (2 Cor. 3:18). Having a revelation of the exceeding greatness of His power will unlock the divine ability in you to walk in extraordinary power. "Exceeding" in the Greek is "huperballo", which literally means to throw above or beyond. May the wisdom of God from this book throw you beyond the natural to walk in the supernatural.

1

The Christian Identity in Christ

There is therefore now no condemnation to them which are in Christ Jesus, who walk not after the flesh, but after the Spirit. For the law of the Spirit of life in Christ Jesus hath made me free from the law of sin and death" (Rom. 8:1-2).

The first two verses of Romans chapter 8 present the core benefits of the believer's identity in Christ. The term in Greek "en Christo" was commonly used by the Apostle Paul to describe who the believers are in Him and the benefits they have received in Him. Verses 1 and 2 mention the phrase "in Christ Jesus". Firstly, the verse identifies their legal position and status before God's holy Law: "There is therefore now no condemnation..."; secondly, it describes negatively and positively the believer's lifestyle or walk: "...who walk not after the flesh, but after the Spirit"; and thirdly, verse 2 identifies the law the believer has come under and the law from which he has been freed: "For the law of the Spirit of life in Christ Jesus hath made me free from the law of sin and death".

The first thing to understand about a believer's judicial status before God is that there is absolutely no condemnation. The term "condemnation" is from the Greek word "katakrino", meaning to pass judgment or sentence against; in other words, to pronounce someone guilty as a result of violating a law. God's law acquits the righteous and condemns the wicked. It is an abomination to God to do the reverse (Prov. 17:15). However, those who are in Christ are counted or declared righteous, not having their own righteousness but the righteousness of Jesus Christ which was charged to our account when He was crucified for us and rose again from the dead (Rom. 4:25). The Bible states,

"Therefore being justified by faith, we have peace with God through our Lord Jesus Christ...For he hath made him to be sin for us, who knew no sin; that we might be made the righteousness of God in him" (Rom. 5:1; 2 Cor. 5:21).

In Christ, we are justified or declared righteous by faith through the finished work and person of Jesus Christ which presents the moral basis for our justification or acquittal. The means by which we obtain it, without the works of the law, is by faith (Rom. 10:9-10). In the work of redemption, our guilt and liability for punishment that properly belonged to us - which is death - was charged to Christ's account to suffer (1 Peter 2:24) and His righteousness which properly belonged to Him, which was "not guilty", was charged to our account. Therefore, the benefits of His sacrificial work were that we were declared to be the righteousness of God in Christ, and have peace with God through the work of the cross (Rom. 5:8). And so no one has any moral or legal right to condemn those whom God has already justified (Rom. 8:33-34). Your past sin that the Devil seeks to bring to your attention has no moral or legal basis to hold you in condemnation, because in Christ, you are a new creation, old things have passed away and all things have become new (2 Cor. 5:17). The old man that used to do those things is dead, crucified and buried with Christ. When Christ rose again from the dead, you were raised with Him to walk in newness of life (Rom. 6:3-6; Eph. 4:22-24). Anytime the enemy comes to condemn and accuse you about your past, overcome him by your word of testimony about what the blood of Jesus Christ has done for you.

Your old identity has passed away in Christ and you now have a new identity in Him; and this new identity tells you that you are a brand new species – a new creation in Christ – and it testifies to the fact that you are the righteousness of God in Him (2 Cor. 5:17, 21); you are God's workmanship – His masterpiece created in Christ Jesus, and God's creative work is perfect, complete, infinitely wise and skilful. His work of creation far surpasses anything that men could design or make. So do not put yourself down or deem yourself as worthless or no good for you are fearfully and wonderfully made (Ps. 139:14). This is true in the natural with the multi-complexity of human cells, organs and diverse functions, but it is even more awesome and wonderful in the realm of the spirit. In Christ Jesus, you are infinitely valuable and priceless; that is why it is important for you to know who you are in Christ so that you can function in the earth as His masterpiece – a manifested son – to reveal the glory of Christ to the world (Rom. 8:19)

We are born-again with the incorruptible life of God in us (Jn. 3:3-8; 1 Peter 1:23). As born again believers, we are capable of living an extraordinary life that glorifies God. We are called to be extraordinary people created to do extraordinary things. Ephesians 2:10 exclaims,

"For we are his workmanship created unto good works, which God hath before ordained that we should walk in them."

The root and essence of the Christian life is about being, not doing. Performing good works are the fruit of Christian living. As a root precedes fruit, so the essence of being, precedes good works. Who you are does not begin with what you do, but what you do begins with who you are. Having a revelation of who you are in Christ will empower you to do the extraordinary in spiritual morality and the miraculous (Jn. 14:12-14; 15:1-16).

In Babylon, Daniel and his three friends, Shadrach, Meshech and Abednego, excelled in knowledge and wisdom above their Gentile peers because they had an excellent spirit (Dan. 1:17-20). The Scriptures tell us about Daniel having

"...an excellent spirit, and knowledge, and understanding, interpreting of dreams, and shewing of hard sentences, and dissolving of doubts, were found in the same Daniel..." (Dan. 5:12).

This is why it is important that every believer is filled with the Spirit (Acts 1:8; 2:1-4) and discover their preordained vocation. Functioning in your vocation will unlock the supernatural potential that was deposited in you by the Spirit. Whether you are called into a fivefold ministry office or called into business, or called to be a mechanic, a schoolteacher, an electrician or solicitor, God, by His Spirit will anoint your abilities and talents to far exceed your fellow-employees and counterparts, which will astound and surprise them to acknowledge that God's wisdom resides in you.

Walking after the Spirit

The last clause of verse 1 of Romans 8 describes the walk of believers in Christ: "...who walk not after the flesh, but after the Spirit." This walk of the believer is described in two aspects: negatively and positively. "Walk", in Scripture signifies one's behaviour, conduct, lifestyle, manner of life or relationship. For example, we are called to live our life by faith; hence, the Christian's life is described as a walk of faith (2 Cor. 5:7). And as regards relationship, the Bible states,

"As ye have therefore received Christ Jesus the Lord, walk ye in him" (Col. 2:6).

Amos 3:3 also says,

"Can two walk together, except they be agreed?"

Therefore, the descriptive clause of Romans 8:2 states that the believers in Christ, who do not walk after the flesh but after the Spirit, are those whose lifestyle, behaviour or manner of life is not in agreement or in conformity to the fleshly lifestyle but is acquiescent to the direction, promptings and character of the Holy Spirit. The Apostle Paul uses the term "flesh" in a moral and ethical sense to refer to the unregenerate, sinful nature of man who is flesh. His walk, conduct, manner of life and thought-life are antithetical to the Spirit.

Verse 2 tells us why the believer in Christ is not under condemnation because:

"...the law of the Spirit of life in Christ Jesus hath made me free from the law of sin and death."

The writer personalises this verse to himself, that he has been made free from the law of sin and death, a stark difference to his personal experience of bondage to sin in chapter 7, prior to believing in Jesus the Messiah. His experience of freedom is also the inheritance of every believer in Christ. Since the law of the Spirit of life is in Christ and every believer is also in Christ, those who are in Him come under the law of the Spirt of life and have been made free from the law of sin and death; that is why there is no more condemnation or judgment against them.

There are two laws mentioned that are antithetical to each other: the law of the Spirit of life that brings liberty and the law of sin and death that brings sin, bondage and death. As the natural realm functions by established laws, for example, gravity, the rising and setting of the sun or agriculture, so does the realm of the spirit. In fact, the laws of nature teach us about the laws of the Spirit, for the former is a reflection of the latter. God has designed creation this way to show us how the invisible world operates. The Bible states,

"Because that which may be known of God is manifest in them; for God hath shewed it unto them. For the invisible things of him from the creation of the world are clearly seen, being understood by the things that are made, even his eternal power and Godhead; so that they are without excuse" (Rom. 1:19-20).

This is why the nature of Hebrew wisdom draws from nature and creation to teach us about certain spiritual principles of morality, ethics and truths about God. It is essentially practical and easily lends itself to the use of parables, similes, proverbs, dreams and symbolic language to teach spiritual truths, e.g., parable of the sower (Matt. 13); teaching about the tongue (Jam. 3)

Like natural laws, these two laws, the law of the Spirit of life and the law of sin and death, are consistent. As a human being, you will either live under the law of the Spirit of life, or you will live under the law of sin and death; you only have two options: either you receive Christ and live under the law of the Spirit of life or reject Christ and live without Him under the law of sin and death. There are only two alternatives. These two antithetical laws are also mentioned in the Old Testament.

In the book of Genesis, there were two trees mentioned in the Garden of Eden: the tree of life, and the tree of the knowledge of good and evil; the former represented the law of life and the latter the law of sin and death. The one that was chosen was done at the expense of the other; you cannot embrace both. Adam decided to eat of the tree of knowledge of good and evil and forfeited the tree of life (Gen. 2:16-17; 3:6-7, 22, 24).

The book of Deuteronomy also records the presentation of these two opposing laws for Israel to make the right choice,

"See, I have set before thee this day life and good, and death and evil...I call heaven and earth to record this day against you, that I have set before you life and death, blessing and cursing: therefore choose life, that both thou and thy seed may live" (Deut. 30:15, 19).

The law of the Spirit of life is designated as life, good and blessing; the law of sin and death is described as death, evil and cursing. And Deuteronomy 28 lists the things that are catego-

The Christian Identity in Christ

rised under the law of life and the law of death. God exhorts His people to choose life so that they may live.

Under the New Covenant, Jesus Christ is the one we must choose and continue to serve so that we may appropriate the benefits - the law of the Spirit of life, which is only in Christ Jesus. The law of the Spirit of life in Christ Jesus summarises the things that belong to the believer initiated by the new birth (Jn. 3:3, 5). To the believer in Christ belongs life, peace, health, blessings, prosperity, protection, authority, power, joy and more. I began verse 1 of Romans chapter 8 with who we are in Christ – that we are the righteousness of God in Christ because there is no condemnation; and then verse 2 sums up what we have in Him. Let us endeavour to search the Scriptures to find out more about what it means to be a new creation in Christ

2

The Law of Works Versus the Righteousness of Faith

For what the law could not do, in that it was weak through the flesh, God sending his own Son in the likeness of sinful flesh, and for sin, condemned sin in the flesh. That the righteousness of the law might be fulfilled in us, who walk not after the flesh, but after the Spirit" (Rom. 8:3-4).

In the opening verses, the Apostle Paul presents the inability of the Mosaic Law to save and the effectual necessity of God sending His own Son to set men free from the bondage of sin and death. As a matter of fact, God never designed for the Law to have saving power, hence the phrase, "For what the law could not do...". The Scriptures present several aspects as to what the Law could not do: it could not make the worshippers perfect as to their conscience (Heb. 10:1-2); it could not take away sins (v3-4); it could not give life (Rom. 7:10; 2 Cor. 3:6); the Law could not fulfil its righteousness in us (Rom 8:3-4); it could not set us free from sin's innate power within us (Rom. 7:7-25; 8:3).

According to the last statement as to what the Law could not do, the Apostle Paul shows us why the Law could not do anything with regard to man's salvation. It reads,

"For what the law could not do, in that it was weak through the flesh..." (v3a).

The Law could not do anything with regard to man's salvation because it [the Law] was weak through the flesh. It was weak to do anything because of the inner sinful character and failure of man to live up to its required standards of righteousness and holiness. In this statement lies the root cause of why the Law was given. The Law was not given to empower man to obey it, but rather to show that man was weak and could not obey it. Therefore, the Law was weak, not in itself, but by virtue of the morally corrupt and unregenerate nature of man, who is referred to as "flesh". In this respect, the purpose of the Law was given: 1) because of transgressions (Gal. 3:19); 2) that the offence might abound (Rom. 5:20); 3) by the Law is the knowledge of sin (Rom. 3:20; 7:7); the Law imputes guilt to the sinner (Rom. 5:13).

The Apostle Paul, trained as a Jewish scholar in the Law, came to understand vividly what sin was, by the Law of the Ten Commandments. Therefore, attempting to obey the commandments perfectly, he failed miserably to keep them and fulfil the righteousness of the Law, because the sin nature was inherent in him. He acknowledges that the Law is holy, just and good (Rom. 7:7, 12), but rather he is enslaved by the sin that dwells within him. The sin nature in Him takes advantage or ascendancy over him by his knowledge of sin revealed in the Law. He confirms,

"For we know that the law is spiritual: but I am carnal, sold under sin. For that which I do I allow not: for what I would, that do I not; but what I hate, that do I. If then I do that which I would not, I consent unto the law that it is good. Now then it is no more I that do it, but sin that dwelleth in me. For I know that in me (that is in my flesh,) dwelleth no good thing: for to will is present with me; but how to perform that which is good I find not" (Rom. 7:14-18).

Paul describes the Law as being spiritual because it is holy, just and good; but identifies himself as carnal: used ethically and morally to depict the sinful, unregenerate man governed by his fleshly appetites in opposition to the Spirit of God. His usage of both terms: "spiritual" and "carnal" are ethical in nature. The word "carnal" is from the Greek rendering "sarkikos" which is derived from "sarx", meaning Flesh. Paul qualifies this by saying that He was sold under sin. He further stresses concerning that which he does, he does not approve: "For that which I do I allow [Gk dokimazo, approve] not." The meaning of this statement is reiterated in the subsequent verses of the passage. The sins Paul desired not to do, he did, acknowledging that it was the sin that dwelt in him. The sin in him was aroused by the holy commandments contained in the Law, and brought to his attention, the consciousness of sin. Paul's experience describes what it means to be under the Law.

There are several aspects to living under the Law: 1) being under moral obligation to keep the whole Law (Ja. 2:10-11); 2) failing to fulfil the righteousness of the Law by works (Rom. 3:20; Gal. 2:16); 3) living under the curse of the Law (Gal. 3:10); 4) living under its ceremonial and sacrificial system of which there is a remembrance of sins (Heb. 10:1-4). These are the fruit of trying to obtain righteousness by the works of the Law.

The phrase "works of the Law" is outwardly conforming to a set of rules and norms without the heart being changed. It is seeking to obey the Law through your own strength and effort with the root of sin inside. Metaphorically, it is like trying to produce fruit without a tree. Additionally, the law of works is propelled by fleshly boasting and pride desiring not to humble itself and give glory to God (Rom. 3:27). No man can be justified or declared not having sinned by the works of the Law. Before having a knowledge of sin by the Law, it shows you that you have already sinned prior to knowing the Law. It shows up what was already there; sin appears sinful to the conscience by the knowledge of the Law (Rom. 7). It is impossible to be justified by the deeds of the Law because all have sinned and come short of the glory of God (Rom. 3:23). Nevertheless, we have hope of pleasing God – of being declared righteous in the sight of God – and that is by faith in Jesus Christ and His sacrificial work.

Because the Law was impotent through the flesh, God sent His own Son in the likeness of sinful flesh; and sin being His purpose for being sent, condemned sin in the flesh. This statement in verse 3 unveils the purpose of why the Divine essence – His own Son – was incarnate in human flesh, taking upon Himself the humanity of sinful flesh. The passage is not saying that God's Son partook of our sinful nature but rather partook of our humanity and yet without sin (Heb. 4:15). In His humanity, God sent Him into the world for the ultimate purpose of condemning sin in the flesh. The Scripture affirms,

"he that committeth sin is of the devil, for the devil sinneth from the beginning. For this purpose the Son of God was manifested, that he might destroy the works of the devil" (1 Jn. 3:8).

The primary focus of this verse is sin. That is why it says at the outset that he who commits sin is of the Devil because he sinned from the beginning and is still sinning today. And for this reason the Son of God came to destroy the works of the Devil, particularly his works of sin in flesh – humanity. The root of his works is sin, the fruit of his works is death which includes sickness, diseases, physical deformities and demise, poverty, depression, misery, demonic oppression etc. Once the root of sin is destroyed, its fruit has no basis on which to thrive, for when, by one man, sin entered the world, death also entered by sin, and so death passed upon all men (Rom. 5:12). God's condemnation of sin included its destruction. If He condemned every sin under the Law, every human being would have been destroyed by His fiery indignation simply because sin can only be condemned and punished in the flesh. It cannot be destroyed apart from the person who perpetrated the thought, the motive, the lust or the overt act. Sin does not exist by itself, it only exists in the persons who perpetuate it. And for this reason God's mercy and longsuffering kept the absolute power of the Law in abeyance for man's sake until the Son of God came upon whom its absolute power and justice would be felt.

So Jesus Christ, the spotless, sinless Son of God, tasted the full wrath of the Law for every person. God condemned, punished and destroyed sin in the flesh of His Son so that all sin would be destroyed in the flesh of every one who believes in Jesus Christ (1 Peter 2:24; Rom. 6:1-6; 2 Cor. 5:14-15, 17). By our union with Him, when He was crucified, we were crucified with Him; when He was buried, we were buried with Him; when He rose again from the dead, we were raised together with Him; and when He ascended to heaven to sit at the right hand of God, we also

The Law of Works Versus the Righteousness of Faith

ascended with Him to sit at the right hand of the throne of God (amazing as it sounds!) (Eph. 1:20-21; 2:5-6).

God charged the legal guilt, liability and punishment for our sins to His Son, and His Son's righteousness – never having sinned was charged to us, the believers, who have put our trust in Christ and His finished work. The benefit of God condemning sin in His Son's body is stated in verse 4,

"That the righteousness of the law might be fulfilled in us, who walk not after the flesh, but after the Spirit."

This verse presents righteousness as the antithesis to condemnation; that is why the opening of chapter 8 begins with the truth that there is no condemnation to those who are in Christ Jesus because the righteousness of the Law has been fulfilled in us.

The Greek term for righteousness in this passage is "dikaioma" and it comprehensively signifies the concrete expression of righteousness. It is a declaration that a person or thing is righteous, outlined in His ordinances and precepts, hence signifying the righteous requirements or demands of the Law (Lk. 1:6; Rom. 2:26). It also denotes a sentence of acquittal by which the righteous Judge acquits men of their guilt. Conversely, "dikaioma" also refers to the righteous demand for punishment and retribution (Rom. 2:26).

Jesus fulfilled the righteousness of the Law on our behalf by 1) His total and perfect obedience to His Father's commandments (Jn. 8:29, 46; 11:15:10; Rom. 5:18-19; Phil. 2:8; Heb. 5:8). Also, He fulfilled the righteousness of the Law by satisfying its righteous demands for justice against sin through His sacrificial death on the cross (Is. 53; Rom. 3:25-26; 1 Jn. 4:10). Therefore, we are declared righteous without the deeds of the Law by faith in what Jesus Christ accomplished for us. And again, verse 4 concludes with the reiteration of verse 1: "...who walks not after the flesh, but after the Spirit." The walk, conduct and behaviour of believers in Christ are according to the Spirit. In other words, their lives are in accordance with the Holy Scriptures inspired by the Holy Spirit (2 Peter 1:29-21). Obedience to the Scriptures is walking after the Spirit.

3

Having the Mind of the Spirit

"For they that are after the flesh do mind the things of the flesh, but they that are after the Spirit the things of the Spirit. For to be carnally minded is death; but to be spiritually minded is life and peace. Because the carnal mind is enmity against God: for it is not subject to the law of God, neither indeed can be. So then they that are in the flesh cannot please God" (Rom. 8:5-8).

In the opening verses lie the key to walking after the Spirit or walking after the flesh. Remember how I stated previously that the terms "flesh" and "Spirit" are used in an ethical and moral sense to depict the unregenerate man's sinful nature and appetites in contrast to the regenerate man's new nature born of the Spirit, whose desires follow the promptings and dictates of the Holy Spirit (Gal. 5:15-25; Jn. 3:3-6); one is the antithesis of the other.

The Apostle Paul presents a specific order to one's manner of walk in life, whether for good or evil. You cannot avoid this order-principle. Every person will operate under it; it is inevitable. You can only choose whether to use it for the Kingdom of God or for the kingdom of darkness. Solomon, king of Israel, uttered this truth about 3000 years ago saying,

"For as he thinketh in his heart, so is he..." (Prov. 23:7a).

The order-principle of life is this: the way you think will determine what you become, and what you become will determine how you walk in life. Where the mind goes, the person will follow, for you are what you think. If you want to change your walk, you will have to change your thinking. This is the order-principle for changing your life. The opening scripture informs us that those who walk after the flesh do set their minds on fleshly things and those who walk after the Spirit do set their minds on spiritual things. A person's behaviour or conduct is rooted in his thinking. If you desire to live a life that is pleasing to God, your thought process has to change. The more you think on spiritual things, the stronger your walk according to the Spirit will be; the greater your focus on the things of the flesh, the stronger your fleshly walk will be. Change your focus and you will change the direction of your life. I exhort you to walk according to the Spirit by becoming spiritually minded. Colossians 3:1-2 instructs,

"If ye then be risen with Christ, seek those things which are above, where Christ sitteth on the right hand of God. Set your affection on things above, not on things on the earth."

Because we are risen with Christ to walk in newness of life (Rom. 7:6), we are encouraged to seek or pursue those heavenly things – the things of the Spirit - where Christ is seated at the right hand of God, not fleshly or earthly things. The next verse instructs how to do this: by setting your affections on things above. In the Greek rendering, the term "affection" is "phroneo", meaning to think or be minded in a certain way; to think of or be mindful of. It signifies moral interest; hence, the mind of the flesh and the mind of the Spirit. This Greek term is also used in Romans 8:5 as mind, for those who walk after the flesh and who walk after the Spirit.

In practical terms, how do you set your thinking on spiritual things as opposed to earthly and fleshly things? It is important to note that God has given us His Word to shape our thinking. We begin this process of shaping our minds to line up with heavenly things by reading, studying, hearing and confessing the Word of God. You cannot think on something you do not know. You must obtain that information first before meditating on it.

The Word of God is a literary representation and description of all heavenly and spiritual realities. It is the window, mirror or telescope by which we are able to see into the realm of the spirit. And what we see needs to be thought on, pondered and meditated on until we understand and be firmly focused on the unseen. It then becomes more real than the things that are seen. In 1 Timothy 4:13, 15, it states,

"Till I come, give attendance to reading, to exhortation, to doctrine...Meditate upon these things; give thyself wholly to them; that thy profiting may appear to all."

This order is presented by the Apostle Paul to Timothy. He is instructed to give attendance to reading, exhortation and doctrine (teaching). Then to meditate upon those things he gave attendance to so that his spiritual progress may appear to all men. This is how to think on the things of the Spirit since they are tantamount to what is contained in the Word inspired by the Spirit of God (2 Peter 1:21).

Whatever situation you find yourself in that contradicts the Word, there is a promise in the Word that can change it, whether it be sickness, financial lack, depression, a bad temper, fear, hatred or an addiction. There is a word from the Bible that will cover any situation or character flaw in your life. Take the Word and search thoroughly to find the scriptures that are specifically relevant to what you want to see change. Meditate and ponder those scriptures daily, rolling them over in your mind. Then reinforce your meditation by speaking those verses to yourself, for in so doing, you will pull down and destroy those strongholds: ungodly thought-patterns in your mind. The book of Joshua states,

"This book of the law shall not depart out of thy mouth; but thou shalt meditate therein day and night, that thou mayest observe to do according to all that is written therein: for then thou shalt make thy way prosperous, and then thou shalt have good success" (Joshua 1:8).

Here lies the strategy for prosperity and good success: do not let the Word of God depart out of your mouth. To have it in your mouth is to speak it forth consistently. Furthermore, to speak forth the Word continually is to meditate on it day and night. Meditation means to ponder and to mutter. By doing these, you will destroy demonic strongholds and replace them with righteous thought-patterns that will determine the choices you make, change your behaviour and reshape your destiny. Renewing your mind through the employment of this discipline of meditation will cause you to observe to do all that is written in the Word of God. Changing the way you think will transform your behaviour and prove the will of God for your life, for then you will make your way prosperous and have good success. All of this is reiterated by the Apostle Paul in Romans 12:2,

"And be not conformed to this world: but be ye transformed by the renewing of your mind, that ye may prove what is that good, and acceptable, and perfect will of God."

To guarantee that you walk according to the Spirit and not fall back into the lifestyle of the flesh is to ensure that your mind is stayed on the things of God (Is. 26:3; Col. 3:1-2). Christians backslide into their former lifestyle because at some point in their Christian journey, they began to think on their former life of sin which consequently created the opportunity for them to return to the world. The Bible makes a statement about the patriarchs who died in faith because they endured unto the end:

"And truly, if they had been mindful of that country from whence they came out, they might have had opportunity to have returned. But now they desire a better country, that is, an heavenly: wherefore God is not ashamed to be called their God: for he hath prepared for them a city" (Heb. 11:15-16).

The reason the patriarchs did not return to their homeland from where they came out is because they did not set their thoughts upon it, therefore, they could not succumb to the temptation to return. The devil cannot tempt you with something you are not thinking on. Your flesh would have to be fed adequately enough for the devil to tempt you to sin. Also, their minds were not focused on their homeland because their thoughts were already occupied with the heavenly country (Heb. 11:10, 13-14). Their mouths revealed where their hearts were focused - that heavenly city - and reinforced it with their words. They meditated, pondered and confessed that they were strangers and pilgrims on the earth (v13),

"For they that say such things declare plainly that they seek a country" (v14).

The way not to entertain your thoughts on earthly things is to occupy your mind on spiritual things reinforcing them in your heart by words, for it cannot be achieved by merely not resisting to think on ungodly thoughts. Rather, it is the replacement of those thoughts with heavenly thoughts that brings the change.

The first generation of Israelites, who came out of Egypt failed to enter the Promised Land because their own words revealed that the thoughts of their hearts were still back in Egypt (Ex. 14:11-12; 16:2-3; 17:2-3; 32:1-6; Num. 11:4-6, 18, 20; 14:1-4; 16:13-14; 21:5). Because their minds were back in Egypt, focused on its pagan and ungodly culture, they could not please God. His will was not for them to be in Egypt but to enter the Promised Land. Their Egyptian minds were carnal; therefore, they could not please God and the consequence of this led to death. Romans 8:6 tells us that to be carnally minded is death but to be spiritually minded is life and peace. In the original Greek grammatical construction of this verse it states that the mind of the flesh is death, but the mind of the spirit is life and peace. Verses 5 and 7 reveal four important truths about the carnal mind: 1) it produces death; 2) it is at enmity with God; 3) it is not subject or submissive to the Law of God; 4) it has no moral or spiritual power to do so. To please God, you must change your mind from carnal thoughts to spiritual thoughts by renewing your mind. Starve the flesh of carnal thoughts and feed the spiritual man with godly thoughts from the Word of God. The Apostle exhorts us:

"...put ye on the Lord Jesus Christ, and make no provision for the flesh, to fulfil the lusts thereof" (Rom. 13:14).

The Greek word for "provision" gives a clear understanding of how one can make provision for the flesh to fulfil its lusts. The Greek rendering is "pronoia", meaning forethought, to think beforehand. Hence, to fulfil the flesh with its lusts requires you to think on the things of the flesh before fulfilling its desires and acting accordingly. This is how one makes provision for the flesh. Therefore starve the flesh of ungodly things in the form of thoughts, words or images that come to us through friendships, television, internet, newspapers and books, music etc. Refuse to be entertained by these if their messages and images do not correspond with the truth of God's Word. Instead use all resources including technological inventions to feed your spirit with the Word of God and build and maintain spiritual mindedness that leads to life and peace.

4

Life in the Spirit

So then they that are in the flesh cannot please God. But ye are not in the flesh, but in the Spirit, if so be that the Spirit of God dwell in you. Now if any man have not the Spirit of Christ, he is none of his" (Rom. 8:8-9).

To understand what it means to be in the Spirit, you will need to know two things: 1) the historical background to the life of the Early Church in the book of Acts which provides context to the letters to the churches; 2) the theological and doctrinal context in the light of the apostolic teachings within the New Testament books. In the mouth of two or three witnesses, let truth be established (Matt. 18:16). These are the two principles upon which I will discuss the biblical meaning of being in the Spirit.

The Apostle Paul states in verse 8 that those who are in the flesh cannot please God. In referring to the morally and spiritually corrupt nature of man, who is flesh, he has no inherent power to please God. All who have not received and believed the truth of the Gospel that they might be born again, are incapable of pleasing God because their unregenerate nature is incompatible with God. That is what it means to be in the flesh. Their interests, desires and thinking are only geared for earthly, carnal and ungodly things (Rom. 8:5).

However, the Apostle makes a contrast between the unsaved and the believers in Christ, called the Church. He says, "But ye are not in the flesh, but in the Spirit..." (v9a). According to what context did the apostle define the concept of being in the Spirit? The answer lies in the following clause of the verse, as a condition to being in the Spirit. It states,

"But ye are not in the flesh, but in the Spirit, IF SO BE THAT THE SPIRIT OF GOD DWELL IN YOU..."

The scripture clearly states that those who are in the Spirit have achieved this because the Spirit of God is dwelling in them. We also have a second witness from the epistle to the Galatians chapter 3:2-3:

"This only would I learn of you, RECEIVED YE THE SPIRIT by the works of the law, or by the hearing of faith? Are ye so foolish? HAVING BEGUN IN THE SPIRIT, are ye now made perfect by the flesh?"

According to the context of these verses, to begin in the Spirit implies that you have had to receive the Spirit. In the mouth of two witnesses, let truth be established.

Now, do we understand what the terms: "Spirit of God dwell in you" and "Received ye the Spirit" are referring to? To answer this, we must examine the historical context of the book of Acts that narrates and records the spiritual experiences and events of the

Early Church empowered by the Holy Spirit; hence the book being described by many bible scholars as the Acts of the Holy Spirit.

Just prior to Jesus ascension into heaven, he made a commandment to His disciples recorded in Acts 1:4-5:

"And being assembled together with them, commanded them that they should not depart from Jerusalem, but wait for the promise of the Father which, saith he, ye have heard of me. For John truly baptized with water; but ye shall be baptized with the Holy Ghost not many days hence."

Jesus' command to His disciples was to wait in Jerusalem for the promise of the Father which is identified in the following verse, to be the baptism with the Holy Spirit. This promise, Jesus said, "Ye have heard of me." In other words Jesus had spoken to His disciples before this concerning the promise of the Holy Spirit in St John 14, 15 and 16. In one passage, He announced,

"And I will pray the Father, and he shall give you another Comforter that he may abide with you for ever; even the Spirit of truth; whom the world cannot receive, because it seeth him not, neither knoweth him: but ye know him; for he dwelleth with you, and shall be in you" (Jn. 14:16-17).

Jesus declares to His disciples the coming of the Holy Spirit, promised and to be given by the Father. Furthermore, He states how the Holy Spirit was relating to His disciples while He was with them in the flesh, and how the Spirit would relate to them in the future. Jesus confirmed that the Holy Spirit was with them, and how, in the future, He was going to be in them. As born- again disciples of Jesus Christ, clean through His word (Jn. 15:3), the Holy Spirit was with them. But on the Day of Pentecost, the Holy Spirit came to dwell in them. Acts 2:1-4 records,

"And when the day of Pentecost was fully come, they were all with one accord in one place. And suddenly there came a sound from heaven as of a rushing mighty wind, and it filled all the house where they were sitting. And there appeared unto them cloven tongues like as of fire, and it sat upon each of them. And they were all filled with the Holy Ghost, and began to speak with other tongues, as the Spirit gave them utterance."

In this account, the Holy Spirit came to dwell in Jesus' disciples in fulfilment of His words in St John 14:17. And so confirm the Apostle Paul's words to the Corinthians:

"Know ye not that ye are the temple of God, and that the Spirit of God dwelleth in you...What? Know ye not that your body is the temple of the Holy Ghost which is in you, which ye have of God, and ye are not your own" (1 Cor. 3:16; 6:19)?

When the Apostle Paul addressed the churches in his letter, he was addressing Spirit-filled believers according to the historical events and spiritual experiences in the book of Acts. After souls were saved through the preaching of the gospel, they were prayed for to receive the baptism in the Holy Spirit with the evidence of speaking in tongues. If the apostles met any believers who had not received the Holy Spirit, they were prayed for (Acts 2:38-39; 8:14-19; 9:17; 10:44-47; 19:1-7). According to these passages, the baptism with the Holy Spirit is called "receiving the gift of Holy Ghost" (Acts 2:38) or "receiving the Holy Ghost" (Acts 8:15, 17; 10:47; 19:2). Both of these terms: the "Spirit of God dwelling in you" and "receiving the Holy Spirit", identify the experience of being baptised in the Holy Spirit with the initial evidence of speaking in languages supernaturally according to church history in the book of Acts. So when Paul applies Romans 8:9 to the Christian church at Rome, he is addressing it to a Spirit-filled church, baptised in the Holy Spirit and who spoke in tongues.

The last clause of Romans 8:9 states, "...if any man have not the Spirit of Christ, he is none of his." In context, this statement denotes the same experience I referred to previously: namely, the baptism with the Holy Spirit. Since Paul was addressing Spirit-filled believers, those who he referred to as not having the Spirit because they are not His, describes the unbelievers of the ungodly world system, whom Jesus said, "cannot receive, because it seeth him not, neither know him" (Jn. 14:17). Paul, like Jesus, was making a distinction between the world and the Church in his day. Jude, in his epistle, made a similar proclamation regarding unbelievers in contrast to Christians to whom he was addressing his letter:

"But, beloved, remember ye the words which were spoken before of the apostles of our Lord Jesus Christ; How that they told you there should be mockers in the last time, who should walk after their own ungodly lusts. These be they who separate themselves, sensual, having not the Spirit. But ye, beloved, building up yourselves on your most holy faith, praying in the Holy Ghost" (1:17-20).

Jude reiterates the words of the apostles that there would be mockers in the last time, who would walk according to their own lusts, and identifies them as not having the Spirit. He then makes a contrast with the Christian believers by using the words "but ye beloved". In so doing, he alludes to the fact that they have the Spirit, because he exhorts them in the following clause of verse 20 to build themselves up on their most holy faith by praying in the Holy Spirit, which actually means to pray in tongues – the initial evidence of the baptism with the Holy Spirit (1 Cor. 14:2, 14-15; Eph. 6:18).

The Early Church in the time of the Apostle Paul were united in doctrine and practice regarding the baptism in the Holy Spirit and the ministry of praying in tongues; unlike the Church today which is divided and in disagreement concerning the baptism with the Holy Spirit, His supernatural gifts in the Church and other relevant subjects. You have different groups who believe tongues and the gifts of the Spirit have ceased, and others who believe that they are for today. And this is why I deemed it appropriate to interpret Romans 8: 9 in the light of the belief and practice of the Early Church. Although not all believers in Christ embrace the doctrine and practice of speaking in tongues as evidence of the baptism with the Holy Spirit, I do believe that they are saved, having the Spirit with them (Jn. 14:17), and belong to Jesus Christ. However, in these last days, God is restoring back to His Church the prevalence and common practice of the New testament pattern as was demonstrated in the book of Acts, and that all true believers will embrace the power of living in the Spirit of which the threshold is the baptism with the Holy Spirit (Acts 1:8; Rom. 8:9; Gal. 3:2-3).

5

The Impact of the Divine Life in the Human Body

"And if Christ be in you, the body is dead because of sin; but the Spirit is life because of righteousness. But if the Spirit of him that raised up Jesus from the dead dwell in you, he that raised up Christ from the dead shall also quicken your mortal bodies by his Spirit that dwelleth in you" (Rom. 8:10-11).

Christ came to provide redemption for the whole man – spirit, soul and body (1 Thes. 5:23). He also came to make alive, through the new birth, the spirit that was dead in trespasses and sins (Ezek. 36:25-26; Jn. 3:3-8; Eph. 2:1, 5; Tit. 3:5); to save the soul – its will and desires – through the renewing of our minds (Heb. 10:39; Ja. 1:21; 5:20); and to redeem the body through divine healing and ultimately culminating in the transfiguration and resurrection at the second coming of Jesus Christ (Ex. 15:26; Deut. 7:15; Is 53:4-5; Matt. 8:16-17; 1 Peter 2:24; 3 Jn. 1:2). Anything short of this is not the true Gospel. If the fall of man affected him holistically, it logically makes sense for God to redeem him from sin to the same degree.

Salvation is basically the administration of divine life in spirit, soul and body. It is the purpose why Jesus came, and he affirmed,

"The thief cometh not, but for to steal, and to kill, and to destroy: I am come that they might have life, and that they might have it more abundantly" (Jn. 10:10).

Jesus contrasts the purpose of His work to that of the work of the thief called the Devil. Christ came to give life abundantly; Satan comes as a thief to take life by stealing, killing and destroying. The stealing, the killing and destroying that you can see in this world are evidence that Satan, the god of this age, is behind every destructive work. But Jesus came to destroy the works of the Devil (1 Jn. 3:8) and give eternal life to everyone who believes in Him.

"For God so loved the world, that he gave his only begotten Son, that whosoever believeth in him should not perish, but have everlasting life" (Jn. 3:16).

The divine life in the Greek rendering is "zoe", translated as "life" in the New Testament and is used to denote the life-principle; life in the absolute sense, the very essence of who God is in Himself, and that life was manifested in His Son and ministered to others by His Spirit (Jn. 1:2; 5:26; 11:25; Rom. 8:2, 11). Christ does not give life to the believer apart from Himself; He is Life (1 Jn. 1:1-2) and when you have Jesus Christ, you have eternal life as an actual present possession. The bible states,

"And this is the record, that God HATH GIVEN to us eternal life, and this life is in his Son. He that HATH the Son HATH life; and he that hath not the Son of God hath not life" (1 Jn. 5:11-12).

The Apostle Paul in the opening verses of this chapter, declares the promise of the impact of the divine life on the believers' mortal bodies. He begins by saying,

"And if Christ be in you, the body is dead because of sin; but the Spirit is life because of righteousness. But if the Spirit of him that raised up Jesus from the dead dwell in you, he that raised up Christ from the dead shall also quicken your mortal bodies by his Spirit that dwelleth in you" (v10-11).

Now concerning the impact of divine life on the mortal body, the resultant effect is divine healing and divine health. They are manifestations of the life of God administered by the Holy Spirit – the law of the Spirit of life functioning in the physical body (Rom. 8:2; Prov. 4:22). God's will is for your body to be quickened by His Spirit. The Greek word for "quicken" is "zoopoieo", meaning to make alive. This word conveys the truth that God will make alive your mortal bodies by His Spirit who dwells in you. The God-Life impacting on the mortal body will produce divine health, unabated physical strength and perfect function of all the organs and members of the body. God will reverse death in the body that occurred because of sin, whether Adam's sin or your own personal sin.

To activate the divine life in your mortal body, there are several truths in verses 10 and 11 that you need to acknowledge. Philemon 1:6 proclaims,

"That the communication of thy faith may become effectual by the acknowledging of every good thing which is in you in Christ Jesus."

It is all about acknowledging what you already have until what you communicate is working in your life. Communication in the Greek is the word "koinonia", which is akin to the verb "koinoneo", which has two senses to its meaning: 1) to have or receive a share (Rom. 15:27; 1 Peter 2:13); 2) to give a share to, or shares with (Rom. 12:13; Gal. 6:6). Therefore in the communication of our faith, we receive and distribute based on the knowledge of every good thing in us in Christ Jesus. Hence the practice of faith is to meditate and communicate so that your faith works (Josh. 1:8; 1 Tim. 4:15). To fellowship with the Lord in meditation (reception) and communication (prayer) connects you to the working power of God through faith (Eph. 3:20).

Verse 10 states, "And if Christ be in you…" That is the revelation knowledge we must have and feed on for He is the Life-Source, the resurrection and the life (Jn. 11:25). You do not need to go anywhere to obtain this Life; this Life is already in you for Christ is your Life (Col. 3:4). And that Christ who is Eternal Life is living in us. When you were born again, you received eternal life into your spirit. Christ does not give life apart from Himself; when you received Life into you, you also received Him in your spirit. And so the mystery of God is this: "Christ in you, the hope of glory" (Col. 1:27). Christ, the Life-Giver is living in you. You already have victorious, overcoming life on the inside of you. The Scripture attests,

"Ye are of God, little children, and HAVE OVERCOME them: because greater is he that is IN YOU than he that is in the world" (1 Jn. 4:4).

We are already overcomers because His overcoming life is resident in us. We have been made partakers of his victorious and triumphant life, joined to the Lord as one spirit (1 Cor. 6:17). The only overcoming you are supposed to do is to maintain what you already have by overcoming in the fight of faith (1 Tim. 6:12; 5:4-5; Rev. 2:7).

Jesus Christ lives in us as the Life-Giving Spirit. The Apostle Paul supports this truth, saying,

"And so it is written, The first man Adam was made a living soul; the last Adam was made a quickening spirit [life giving Spirit]" (1 Cor. 15:45).

In heaven, Christ sits at the right hand of God in glorified humanity, but in His divine invisible essence, as Life-Giving Spirit, dwells in us in the Person of the Holy Spirit. Hence, Christ is the possessor of Life, but the Holy Spirit is the administrator of that Life to the believer. For Christ to be in you is tantamount to saying that the Spirit of Christ is in you (see v9-10). Thus, the apostle states in the next clause, "...the body is dead because of sin; but the Spirit is life because of righteousness" (v10). What this verse of scripture is saying is that if Christ lives in you, although the body is dead because of sin, the Spirit is life because of righteousness. If while the physical body is dead because it is sick, infirmed, diseased or weak in any of its organs or members, the Spirit who is Life will cause divine Life to emanate from the human spirit into the body that is now dead. This is what happened to Abraham at about 100 years old and Sarah at about 90 who believed in God who quickens or makes alive the dead. The Bible asserts about Abraham,

"And being not weak in faith, he considered not his own body now dead, when he was about an hundred years old, neither yet the deadness of Sarah's womb. He staggered not at the promise of God through unbelief, but was strong in faith, giving glory to God; And being fully persuaded that what he had promised, he was able also to perform. And therefore it was imputed to him for righteousness" (Rom. 4:19-22).

This passage of scripture confirms that there are two aspects of death in the human body; 1) incipient death and 2) ultimate physical death. Incipient death is when the body begins to deteriorate over a short or long period of time, or certain parts of the body are not operating at full capacity or stop functioning altogether (Rom. 4:19; 8:10; Heb. 11:12). Ultimate physical death is when the whole body ceases to function because the life-principle designated as spirit has left the body (Ja. 2:26; Lk. 23:46)

Abraham's body and Sarah's womb were dead, but they believed in Him who quickens or makes alive the dead (Rom. 4:17-19; Heb. 11:11). They spent time considering the promise of God about themselves becoming parents of a multitude of people and refused to consider their present circumstances so that they would become fully persuaded about God's word. Abraham already saw himself as a father of many nations because the promise became so real that to him, it was already accomplished. Therefore, he spoke of himself, in the past tense, as a father of many nations, and like God, calling those things that be not as though they were (Rom. 4:17). The Spirit of God quickened their dead bodies through the righteousness of faith – simply because they believed God (Rom. 4:17, 22; Heb. 11:11). For this to happen to you, recognise that Christ, the Life-Giver is living in you; also, understand that your recreated human spirit has been made alive by His Spirit through the righteousness of faith. That same life will vitalise your mortal body. Verse 11 declares,

"But if the Spirit of Him that raised up Jesus from the dead dwell in you, he that raised up Christ from the dead shall also quicken your mortal bodies by his Spirit that dwelleth in you."

According to the above verse, the quickening of the body to divine health confirms two things: the resurrection of Jesus Christ and the coming of the Holy Spirit. That same Spirit who raised Jesus from the dead has come to dwell in us and He will make alive our mortal bodies. That is the law of the Spirit of life functioning in our physical bodies.

There is a threefold significance to the resurrection of Jesus: 1) a spiritual and moral significance: by His resurrection, we have been raised up with Him to walk in newness of life to live unto righteousness (Rom. 6:3-6; 1 Peter 2:24); 2) an eschatological significance: At Christ's Second Coming, the saints, who are dead, shall be raised bodily from corruption to incorruption and those who are alive shall be changed from mortal to immortality (1 Cor. 15:36-44, 50-55; 3) a physical significance: a quickening of our mortal physical bodies to live in health and strength on this earth.

When the Apostle Paul refers to God quickening the mortal bodies by His Spirit who dwells in us, he was not speaking of our mortal bodies being resurrected or changed from mortality to immortality, for several reasons. Firstly, in the resurrection of the saints, the body which dies and is buried is not the same body with which they are raised to life. Paul writes,

"But some man will say, How are the dead raised up? And with what body do they come? Thou fool, that which thou sowest is not quickened, except it die. And that which thou sowest, thou sowest not that body that shall be, but bare grain, it may chance of wheat, or some other grain...So also is the resurrection of the dead. It is sown in corruption; it is raised in incorruption...It is sown a natural body; it is raised a spiritual body. There is a natural body, and there is a spiritual body" (1 Cor. 15:35-37, 42, 44).

So in the resurrection, the mortal body is not quickened but changed. Secondly, the spiritual body has no need to be made alive for it cannot die. Mortal bodies have need of being made alive because of the curse of death that has entered the world through sin (Rom. 5:12; 8:10). And thirdly, the earthly house of this tabernacle, referring to the mortal body, will eventually dissolve, but we have a building – a spiritual body – not made with human hands reserved for us in heaven (2 Cor. 5:1).

At this present time, we need the life of the Spirit coursing through our mortal bodies so that we can live in health and do the work of the Kingdom effectively. To live in supernatural health, we must give attention to the Word of God for the sake of our health and wellbeing. Proverbs 4:20-22 states,

"My son, attend to my words; incline thine ear unto my sayings. Let them not depart from thine eyes; keep them in the midst of thine heart. For they are life unto those that find them, and health unto all their flesh....."

The Hebrew word for health in this verse is "marpe", and it means remedy, cure or medicine. God's Word is His divine prescription for health and it is literally medicine to all your flesh. The Word of God has the power to cure you of any disease or ailment because it resonates with divine life. He sends His Word and heals (Ps. 107:20). As you give attention to God's Word through reading, listening, meditation and confession, the Holy Spirit who dwells in you will respond in imparting life to your physical body. He responds to divine instructions from God's Word just as He did in creation when God said, "let there be light" (Gen. 1:2-3). The Word of God activates life in your body when you give attention to it. Jesus said that the words that I speak are spirit and life (Jn. 6:63). Put God's Word concerning His healing promises and speak them over your physical body and allow the Spirit of life to quicken your mortal body.

6

Living by the Spirit

"Therefore, brethren, we are debtors, not to the flesh, to live after the flesh. For if ye live after the flesh, ye shall die: but if ye through the Spirit do mortify the deeds of the body, ye shall live" (Rom. 8:12-13).

To reiterate and emphasise the point, the flesh in its usage is not referring to the physical body but alludes to the sinful nature and appetites of unregenerate man in antithesis to God. There are three aspects to the concept of flesh used in a moral and ethical sense. Firstly, it signifies the sinful, hereditary nature of man; secondly, it implies a way of thinking that is contrary to the things of the Spirit; and thirdly, it is the operation of the law of sin and death (Rom. 7:23, 25; 8:2). The solution to these two associated problems is threefold: 1) a sinner by nature must have his inner nature changed by being born again (Eph. 2:1-3; Jn. 3:3-8; Tit. 3:5; 2 Cor. 5:17); 2) he must receive power by the baptism in the Holy Spirit to walk as Jesus walked (Acts 1:8; 2:1-4; Gal. 5:16); and 3) once filled with the Spirit, he must renew his mind by the Word of God (Rom. 12:2; Eph. 4:23; 1 Tim. 4:15; Josh. 1:8). In this chapter, I will be discussing these three points in more detail.

The first clause of the opening verses of this chapter alludes to those who are in Christ Jesus as not being debtors to the flesh, to live after the flesh. The Greek rendering of "debtor" is "opheiletes", meaning one who owes anything to another, primarily with regard to money (Matt. 18:24), and the principle behind it is that one became a servant to the lender, as conveyed by Proverbs 22:7:

"The rich ruleth over the poor, and the borrower is servant to the lender."

So when the term "debtor" is used in a metaphorical sense to describe negatively those who are not debtors to the flesh, it is stating that believers are not servants to the flesh, neither does the flesh have dominion over them. They are under no obligation to live according to its lusts.
Those in Christ Jesus who are dead to sin are freed from it (Rom. 6:6-7). We are freed from its nature, its power and its penalty. Do not let sin have dominion over you because your identity is that you are dead to sin and have been made the righteousness of God in Christ Jesus (2 Cor. 5:21).

God has designated four distinct spiritual experiences concerning how the believer can eradicate sin and the flesh from his walk of faith. They are justification, regeneration, the baptism with the Holy Spirit, and the renewing of the mind. These overcome the effects and consequences of sin in the following three aspects: 1) its guilt and penalty; 2) its nature; 3) its weakness; and 4) its carnal mindset; and also helps the person to develop an understanding of his spiritual identity in Christ

Justification

Justification deals with the removal of guilt and liability for punishment, which is death. Guilt or innocence depicts a person's position and relation before God's righteous and holy Law. When one sins by transgressing the Law, God as Judge imputes or charges guilt to the offender, and if innocent, He charges righteousness - declares and shows someone to be righteous. However, the Bible shows that all have sinned, and therefore, are guilty before God; there is none who does good (Rom. 3:10-11, 19, 23). In the plan of redemption, God sent His Son on whom was charged or imputed the legal guilt and liability of the whole world and His legal righteousness was charged to our account by faith in the sacrificial death of Christ (2 Cor. 5:21. Rom. 5:1). Therefore being justified by faith in His blood, we are saved from the wrath of God (Jn. 3:36; Rom. 5:9).

Regeneration

The relationship between justification and regeneration is that justification has to happen before regeneration can occur. Once the legal transaction has taken place whereby God pronounces a sinner as righteous by his faith in the atoning work of Christ, then God's Spirit makes alive his spirit that was spiritually dead (Eph. 2:1-5), thus changing his nature from sin to righteousness. While justification is imputed righteousness, regeneration is infused righteousness. You are no longer a sinner by nature, but you are created in righteousness and true holiness by the new birth (Jn. 3:3-8; Titus 3:5; 1 Peter 1:23). There is no longer any inbred sin. You become a new creation in Christ Jesus; old things are past away and all things have become new (2 Cor. 5:17). By the new birth, we have become partakers of the divine nature (2 Peter 1:4); no more the sons of disobedience and wrath by nature (Eph. 2:2-3), but are now the children of God (1 Jn. 3:1-2). As Jesus is in heaven, so are we on the earth because we have His righteousness (1 Jn. 4:17). Build your spiritual life on the revelation that you are the righteousness of God in Christ and remove the sin-consciousness from your mind and you will not habitually live in sin. And so confirms the words of the Apostle Paul,

"Awake to righteousness and sin not; for some have not the knowledge of God..." (1 Cor. 15:34).

The Baptism with the Holy Spirit

Verse 13 of Romans 8 intimates why God desires to baptise His people in the Holy Spirit:

"For if ye live after the flesh, ye shall die: but if ye through the Spirit do mortify the deeds of the body, ye shall live."

The purpose of the baptism with the Holy Spirit is to mortify the deeds of the body. The Greek term for "mortify" is "thanatoo", which means to put to death. In the redemptive work of Christ, it was God's act and responsibility to put to death the old man – the sinful nature – through the death of Christ (Rom. 7:4-6). That act of God in the believer has already been accomplished. You may ask the question as to why the believer needs the baptism in the Holy Spirit if the work of putting self to death has been done. It was the legal act of God in Christ to put to death the sinner with Christ and to raise him up to walk in newness of life (Rom. 6:3-6; Col. 3:3, 9-10). However, verse 13 refers to the act and responsibility of the believer to put to death, not the old man that was crucified with Christ, but the deeds of the body by the Spirit, in response to what God accomplished in the work of redemption. Vine attests to this from Romans by stating,

"...in 7:4, "ye were dead" (passive voice), betokens the act of God on the believer, through the Death of Christ; here in 8:13 it is the act of the believer himself, as being responsible to answer to God's act, and to put to death "the deeds of the body" "(1985:85).

The baptism with the Holy Spirit gives us power to mortify – put to death – the deeds of the body. Acts 1:8 states,

"But ye shall receive power, after that the Holy Ghost has come upon you..."

In the Greek, the word for "power" is "dunamis", signifying ability, strength, force or might. We are to use the ability and power of the Spirit to put to death the deeds of our bodies that contradict the spiritual and moral principles of the Word of God.

The essence of Christianity is to live and walk as Jesus walked 1 (Jn. 2:6). In the natural, it is not merely difficult; it is impossible. That is why God gave us His Spirit to enable us to truly represent Him as ambassadors to be and to walk as He walked (1 Jn. 4:17), and we are to do it through the Spirit. It is about activating by faith the life and supernatural ability of the Spirit to live beyond the natural. Our Lord gave us insight into the life of the Spirit-filled believer when He taught the Sermon on the Mount (Matt. 5-7). Its teachings are profound truths that deal not merely with outward conduct, but also with the thoughts, motives and intent of the heart. Its teachings were committed to Christ's apostles to teach other disciples (Matt. 28:19-20).

In another passage, the Apostle Paul gave the divine order on how not to fulfil the lusts of the flesh. He proclaims,

"This I say then, Walk in the Spirit, and ye shall not fulfil the lust of the flesh...But the fruit of the Spirit is love, joy, peace, long-suffering, gentleness, goodness, faith, Meekness, temperance: against such there is no law" (Gal. 5:16, 22-23).

Notice the divine order for the believer to mortify or put to death the deeds of the body. It says first to walk in the Spirit and the by-product is that you will not fulfil the lust of the flesh. The fight of the Spirit-filled believer is not against sin's nature within, for that was eradicated when he was born again, but rather contests against sin as a law of principle in temptation (Rom. 8:2). We overcome the lust of the flesh by sowing to the Spirit. Doing right will prevent you from doing wrong. People do wrong because they have failed to do right. Defeat is only attained by default in the walk of faith when you fail to make spiritual investments in time and service to the law of the Spirit (Gal. 6:7-9). Every deed of the body whether good or evil has a root. If the root is corrupt, the deed will also be corrupt or if the root is holy, the deed will also be holy for every tree will produce after its own kind (Matt. 7:16-20). And the root of every deed begins with a thought.

Renewing of the Mind

Thoughts determine your desires and your desires become the driving force behind your deeds. Thoughts are seeds, the heart is the soil and the fruit it produces are deeds. The way to mortify those ungodly deeds by the Spirit is to sow godly seeds in your heart to counteract unholy thoughts. Changing what you sow will change what you are reaping. Renewing the mind is about replacing old thought-patterns with new thought patterns, and you do that with the Word of God. It is the Word that gives us the correct things to think on. But you cannot think on the right things until you give attendance to reading, exhortation and teaching (1 Tim. 4:13, 15). And the spiritual things you meditate on, the Holy Spirit will process the information to be deposited in your heart. In doing so, you will programme your mind and heart to mortify the deeds of the flesh. What you put in is what you will get out.

The Apostle Paul tells us the things to think on:

"Finally, brethren, whatsoever things are true, whatsoever things are honest, whatsoever things are just, whatsoever things are pure, whatsoever things are lovely, whatsoever things are of good report; if there be any virtue, and if there be any praise, think on these things. Those things which ye have both learned, and received, and heard, and seen in me, do: and the God of peace shall be with you" (Phil. 4:8-9).

As part of our meditation, we are also to speak those things to reinforce our thinking and transform our lives. I am not referring to mere mind over matter, but the spiritual law by which you activate the ability of the Spirit in your life to change those character flaws that are needed. The Bible declares that the tongue is the pen of a ready writer (Ps. 45:1). The ready writer is the Holy Spirit who writes the Word of God not on tablets of stone, but on the fleshly tablets of our hearts (2 Cor. 3:3). Before He can write, you must affirm yourself with the words you want Him to write on your heart. In this, God will bring to pass the words of the prophet,

"And I will put my spirit within you, and CAUSE you to walk in my statutes, and ye shall keep my judgments, and do them" (Ezek. 36:27).

And again,

"For this is the covenant that I will make with the house of Israel after those days, saith the Lord; I will put my laws into their mind, and WRITE THEM IN THEIR HEARTS: and I will be to them a God, and they shall be to me a people" (Heb. 8:10).

7

The Spirit of Adoption

"For as many as are led by the Spirit of God, they are the sons of God. For ye have not received the spirit of bondage again to fear; but ye have received the Spirit of adoption, whereby we cry, Abba, Father" (Rom. 8:14-15).

In the above passage of scripture, the Apostle Paul presents the contrast between the spirit of bondage and the Spirit of adoption. These two antithetical concepts are also shown in the book of Galatians chapter 4 which we will look at further in this chapter.

The Greek word for "bondage" is "douleia", denoting slavery, which refers to the condition of being a slave, and has come to signify all kinds of bondage such as the cursed conditions of creation (Rom. 8:21); the fallen state of man bound by fear (v15); the subjection of man to the fear of death (Heb. 2:15); the condition of being enslaved to the elements and principles of the world (Gal. 4:3); and being in bondage to the Mosaic Law (v24). We have not received the spirit of these things that engender bondage, but we have received the Spirit of adoption by which we cry Abba, Father (v15).

The Greek rendering for "adoption" is "huiothesia" from "huios", a son, and "thesis", a placing; hence the basic meaning is to place or position as a son. The Spirit of adoption is the Holy Spirit which we receive when baptised in the Holy Spirit subsequent to the new birth (Jn. 3:3-8; Acts 1:8; 2:1-4; 8:14-19; 10:44-47; 11:15-16; 19:1-7). Take note that the book of Acts defines the baptism with the Holy Spirit as receiving the Spirit. The Holy Spirit has come to create in believers the realisation of their identity as sons and to act accordingly. Adoption refers to those who have become sons of God, possessing all sonship rights, privileges, inheritance, authority and responsibilities that accompany it.

To understand our adoption as sons, we need to comprehend the ancient laws and cultural practices regarding adoption. Firstly, according to Hebrew, Greek and Roman law, there was a distinction between being children consequent upon birth and being sons by adoption. Secondly, fathers bestowed sonship to their own children. Thirdly, adoption was conferred upon children who became of age and ready to take on responsibility. Fourthly, adoption occurred at an appointed time chosen by a father. Fifthly, while the father's descendant remained a child, in understanding, he was no different from a slave, even though his inherentance was lord of all. These principles teach about our adoption in the realm of the spirit.

We are the children of God by the new birth (Jn. 3:3-8) but sons of God by adoption. St John 1:12-13 states,

"But as many as received him, to them gave he [Gk authority] to become the [Gk children] of God, even to them that believe on

The Spirit of Adoption

his name: Which were born, not of blood, nor of the will of the flesh, nor of the will of man, but of God."

We were given the authority – the divine right – to become the children of God through the new birth, when we believed in His Name: that is, the Name of the only begotten Son of God (Jn. 3:18). Then, based on our identity as the children of God via the new birth, we were adopted as sons of God. The book of Galatians affirms,

"But when the fullness of the time was come, God sent forth his Son, made of a woman, made under the law, To redeem them that were under the law, that we might receive the adoption of sons. And because ye are sons, God hath sent forth the Spirit of his Son into your hearts, crying, Abba, Father. Wherefore, thou art no more a [Gk slave, but a son; and if a son, then an heir of God through Christ" (4:4-7).

The appointed time for our adoption came when God sent His Son, made of a woman and made under the Law, to redeem us from the spirit of bondage that was under the Law, so that we would become sons and no more slaves. Then all who believe in Christ and his sacrificial work are no more slaves, but sons. And because we are sons, God sent the Spirit of His Son into our hearts crying Abba, Father. That is the Spirit of adoption. God baptises us in the Holy Spirit because we are now sons. We are not going to be sons in the future or in the sweet by and by when Jesus returns – a resounding no! We are now free and liberated as sons in this dark and sinful world; no longer bound to the spirit of slavery and fear. You have legal access and freedom to God's throne of grace (Heb. 4:15). Sonship is a freedom to be enjoyed by the believer, in contrast to bondage, for where the

Spirit of the Lord is, there is liberty (2 Cor. 3:17; Rom. 8:15). Authority as children and sons of God gives us freedom of speech and freedom of action to cry Abba, father.

Abba is an Aramaic word transliterated into the Greek language of the New Testament, and is found in Mark 14:36; Romans 8:15 and Galatians 4:6. In a Rabbinical commentary on the Mishna, the traditional teaching of the Jews, it was strictly forbidden for slaves to address the head of the family as Abba. Its usage was almost synonymous to a personal name, in contrast to "Father," with which it is used in conjunction. The term "Father", was an added interpretation introduced with the Greek-speaking Jews. While the term "Father", expresses intelligent comprehension of the relationship, Abba depicts unreasonable trust and reliance (Vine 1985). So our expression to God as Father must entail the recognition of who He is as Father and the childlike trust and confidence in Him that encapsulates our relationship as sons.

There are many Christians who are sons, and do not enjoy their sonship rights and privileges as inheritors. Why is this? The answer lies in Galatians 4:1-3,

"Now I say, that the heir, as long as he is a child differeth nothing from a [Gk slave], though he be lord of all; but is under tutors and governors until the time appointed of the father. Even so we, when we were children, were in bondage [Gk slavery] to the elements of the world."

There are two Greek words that are translated child or children in our English Bible: "teknon" and "nepios." Teknon is akin to tikto, meaning to beget or bear; hence teknon stresses relationship by birth used in the natural and spiritual sense (Jn. 1:12-13).

The Spirit of Adoption

The other word, "nepios", is used to refer to those who are carnal and immature (1 Cor. 3:1; Eph. 4;14; Heb. 5:13). It denotes to be without the power of speech, alluding to the fact that the carnal and immature cannot talk correctly, for out of the abundance of the heart the mouth speaks (Matt. 12:34).

In the above passage of scripture (Gal. 4:1, 3), this word "nepios" is used to speak of one who is carnal, immature and lacks understanding, who is unable to assume the responsibilities and privileges of adoption as an heir, even though he is lord of all. And because he is immature, he need to be under tutors and governors until the appointed time of his adoption set by his father (v2). The Apostle Paul relates this in his epistle, to the spiritual condition of the Jewish people under the Mosaic Law prior to the redemptive work of Messiah. Even though Israel was an heir of the Covenant promises and blessings of adoption. God's people were no different from slaves for they were in bondage to the Law through their carnality and sin and therefore could not enjoy their Abrahamic blessings until the messianic Seed should come at a time appointed by the Father. In the meantime, the Law was a tutor, governor and schoolmaster. The Greek rendering of tutor is "epitropos", literally meaning one to whose care something is committed, such as a guardian (Matt. 20:8; Lk. 8:3).The Greek word for governor is "oikonomos", which literally denotes one who rules a house, and signifies a superior servant responsible for the family housekeeping, the guiding and directing of other servants and the care of children under age. The Greek term for schoolmaster is "paidagogos", which connotes a child leader, a guide, a guardian or trainer of boys. His responsibility was not to impart knowledge but to be responsible for the discipline and general supervision of children's physical and moral wellbeing. The Mosaic Law was for the moral and physical wellbeing and the discipline of the people of Israel as a nation who were spiritual babes, until Christ should come.

Paul, in addressing the Galatian brethren, stated that they were in bondage to the elements of the world (v3); the elementary principles and practices of the world such as the dietary laws, circumcision and ceremonial washings, the feast and Sabbath days, the animal sacrifices and Temple worship, which all have been done away with in Christ (see v9-10; Col. 2:8, 14-16, 20-22). According to the Scriptures, the Law was a guardian, a leader of the spiritually immature to bring them to Christ that they might be adopted as sons. Therefore the Scripture states,

"But before faith came, we were kept under the law, shut up unto the faith which afterward should be revealed. Wherefore the law was our schoolmaster to bring us unto Christ, that we might be justified by faith. But after that faith is come, we are no longer under a schoolmaster. For ye are all the [sons] of God by faith in Christ Jesus" (Gal. 3:23-26).

With regard to the adoption of sons, there is no ethnic, social class or gender distinction that counts when it concerns your sonship rights, blessings, privileges, inheritance, authority and responsibilities, for all are one in Christ, as stated in the verse:

"There is neither Jew nor Greek, there is neither bond nor free, there is neither male nor female: for ye are all one in Christ" (Gal. 3:28).

Why are many Christians not enjoying their rights and inheritance as adopted sons? It is partly for the same reason that Israel as a nation did not attain unto the promise of adoption under the Law: namely, because Israel was a "nepios" – a child in spiritual understanding prior to the coming of Christ (Gal. 4:2). Christians who are carnal and spiritually immature will not enjoy their full sonship rights and inheritance even though they are positioned in Christ as heirs and lords over all, having been given all authority (Jn. 1:12; Lk. 10:19; Mk. 16:17-18); power (Acts 1:8; 2:1-4) and all spiritual blessings (Eph. 1:3). God's people are destroyed, not for lack of these, but for lack of spiritual knowledge (Hos. 4:6), and that is what makes them carnal and spiritually immature. This was true of the Corinthian Church. Paul said,

"And I, brethren, could not speak unto you as unto spiritual, but as unto carnal, even as unto babes [Gk nepios] in Christ. I have fed you with milk, and not with meat: for hitherto ye were not able to bear it, neither yet now are ye able. For ye are yet carnal; for whereas there is among you envying, and strife, and divisions, are ye not carnal and walk as men?" (1 Cor. 3:1-3).

The word "carnal in the Greek is "sarkikos" derived from "sarx", meaning flesh; and in this context, it refers to being controlled by the animal appetites, governed by the senses rather than by the Holy Spirit. Carnality is synonymous by implication, to walking after the flesh. They were carnal in their relationship to the Word and in their relationship to each other. The traits of their carnality were that they had strife, envy and divisions among themselves; a by-product of their immaturity towards the Word of God (v1). They failed to do what the Word was commanding them. Spiritual growth comes through learning and doing the Word, for the Bible states that,

"for every one that useth milk is unskilful in the word of righteousness for he is a babe [Gk nepios]" (Heb. 5:13).

The word "unskilful" in the Greek is "apeiros", which signifies to be without practical experience, and is derived from "a", which is negative, and "peira", denoting trial or experiment. It is not merely in the hearing or learning of the Word that brings growth, it is in the understanding and practical application of the Word that one develops to receive meat as confirmed in the Book of Hebrews:

"But strong belongeth to them that are of full age, even those by reason of USE having their senses EXERCISED to discern both good and evil" (Heb. 5:14).

Begin to use the Word you have learned to mortify the deeds of the body through the power of the Holy Spirit, because you are no more slaves but sons. Start to live and walk as sons of God and begin to enjoy and appropriate your adoption rights of authority and power over the Devil, the flesh and the forces of this world, "for as many as are led by the Spirit of God, they are the sons of God" (Rom. 8:14). According to the scriptural context of the passage, the Spirit continuously leads the sons of God to mortify the deeds of the body (v13) and walk in the fruit of the Spirit (Gal. 5:16-23).

There is no appointed time to become sons like Israel who awaited the appointed time of the Messiah, that time has come and gone; it is now time to put aside the deeds of the flesh and begin to appropriate the fullness of our adoption benefits. We have the legal position of authority as sons, the Spirit of adoption has come to empower us to walk and behave as sons (Acts 1:8; Gal. 5:16).

8

The Significance of Being the Children of God

"The Spirit beareth witness with our spirit, that we are the children of God, And if children, then heirs, heirs of God, and joint-heirs with Christ; if so be that we suffer with him, that we may be also glorified together. For I reckon that the sufferings of this present time are not worthy to be compared with the glory which shall be revealed in us" (Rom. 8:16-18).

I believe that it is extremely important that every Christian understands their spiritual identity as the children of God. The term "child of God" has been used so loosely, almost like a cliché, by many born-again believers because they do not fully understand what Jesus accomplished for us in the work of redemption. Consequently, many Christians have become casualties of war in the fight of faith against the deceptive strategies of the kingdom of darkness (Eph. 6:12; 1 Tim. 6:12). Having revelation knowledge on the very essence of what it means to be the children of God will equip you to live the victorious Christian life that Jesus

Christ purchased with His own blood at the cross of Calvary. In this chapter, I want to unveil the essential truths God has shown me concerning the spiritual benefits of being the children of God in Christ.

There are three foundational truths embodied in the opening scriptural passage; 1) the twofold witness of spiritual identity in the believer (v16); 2) the glorious inheritance of the children of God (v17); and 3) the revelation of the glory of God in the saints (v18). These three principles mentioned in their divine order of events will usher in the manifestation of the sons of God to a groaning creation (v19). This revelation of the sons of God will be dealt with in detail in the next chapter.

The Twofold Witness of Spiritual Identity in the Believer

"The Spirit beareth witness with our spirit, that we are the children of God" (v16).

There are two witnesses in this verse that testify to the truth of our spiritual identity in Christ. They not only testify to the truth but also impart to us the assurance of that truth. Jesus defended Himself before the Jewish leaders regarding His spiritual identity as the Light of the world, saying,

"It is also written in your law, that the testimony of two men is true. I am one that bear witness of myself, and the Father that sent me beareth witness of me" (Jn. 7:17-18).

Jesus applies the law of two witnesses to refer to the testimony of Himself and His Father. Jesus bore witness about Himself as He ministered in word and deed (Lk. 24:19; Acts 1:1) and the Father confirmed who He was by revelation and miracles (Jn. 5:19-20, 30-32, 36; Acts 2:22). This principle is also indicative of the believer who, according to Romans 8:16, has the witness of his spirit and the Spirit of God.

The phrase "beareth witness with" is translated from the Greek word "summartureo", and is used also in Romans 2:15 and 9:1. It means to bear testimony together with; hence the Holy Spirit and our born-again human spirit testifies to the truth that we are the children of God. When we were born again, our human spirit which was spiritually dead in sins and trespasses was made alive and recreated anew by the Holy Spirit (Eph. 2:15; Titus 3:5; Ezek. 36:25-26; 2 Cor. 5:17). And so your regenerated human spirit testifies to the fact that you are a child of God, being confirmed by an inward assurance and knowing. Your redeemed spirit will always speak the truth concerning who you are in Christ, therefore you must stay attuned to your spirit through prayer and the ministry of the Word so that you do not become dull of hearing. The spirit of man is the means by which the Lord guides, counsels and directs our lives. Proverbs 20:27 states

"The spirit of man is the candle of the LORD, searching all the inward parts of the belly."

This is why it is so important for the Spirit-filled believer to pray in tongues because as you do so, your spirit is being activated and given the ascendancy over your soul – the self-conscious part of you. The Apostle Paul states,

"for if I pray in an unknown tongue, my spirit prayeth, but my understanding is unfruitful. What is it then? I will pray with the spirit, and I will pray with the understanding also..." (1 Cor. 14:14-

15a).

Praying in tongues is the most effective and the fastest way of attuning yourself to your spirit. This topic will be explored further in the book. The Holy Spirit is a co-witness to our recreated human spirit, unveiling truth concerning who we are in Christ for He is our teacher (Jn. 14:26). He testifies in our hearts to the fact that we are the children of God and teaches us about its meaning and application to our lives.

The essential implication of what it means to be the children of God is revealed in Ephesians 5:1, "Be ye followers of God as dear children." The key word in this verse is "followers", and its Greek rendering is "mimetes", meaning imitator; it is the Greek word from which we get the English words mime or mimic. So, to be a child of God is to be an imitator of Him. That means to be like God and to act like God, for we have been born of His nature, and that nature is love because the following verse (v2) reads, "And walk in love, as Christ hath also loved us..." To act and behave like God, we must walk in love as dear children. The Greek word for "dear" is agapetos", derived from "agape", which means "love"; and "agapetos" signifies to be loved by God; the divine motivation for becoming the children of God. The Scripture affirms,

"behold what manner of love the Father hath bestowed upon us, that we should be called the [Gk children] of God..." (1 Jn. 3:1a).

As children loved of God, we are to walk in love one towards another and towards our enemies (Lk. 6:27, 35). The Apostle John announces that everyone who loves is born of God and anyone who does not love is not of God for God is love (1 Jn. 4:7-

8). Our spiritual identity is that we are the children of Love, who is God. So, let us walk in love being imitators of God as beloved children.

In Christ, we are children of the Abrahamic blessing and have been delivered from the Adamic curse that belongs to the children of men because Christ was made a curse for us (Gal. 3:13-14). The blessings legally belong to us because being children of God, we are heirs

The Glorious Inheritance of the Children of God

As heirs, we have a twofold relationship with regard to our inheritance: 1) heirs of God; 2) joint-heirs with Christ. God is the Author and Bestower of the inheritance to us as His children. In addition, that inheritance was not bequeathed to us on our own merits, but rather on the merits of Christ. We possess these from God, based on our union and identification with Him. All that has been appointed for Christ, has also been appointed for us because we are in Him. The Hebrew writer affirms that God has appointed Him to be the heir of all things (Heb. 1:2). Everything that Christ possesses, also belongs to the children of God in Him.

There is an aspect of our glorious inheritance that is to be realised in this life, and another that can only be fulfilled in the next. Pertaining to this life, we are heirs of the righteousness of God by faith (Heb. 11:7; Rom. 5:1; 2 Cor. 5:21); we are made partakers of the divine nature (2 Peter 1:4; 1 Jn. 4:17); we have the mind of Christ (1 Cor. 2:16; Phil. 2:5); we have inherited the promise of the Holy Spirit (Acts 1:4-5, 8; 2:1-4; Gal. 3:14); we have inherited His authority over devils, sickness, diseases and infirmities (Matt. 10:1, 8; Mk. 16:17-18); we also possess authority and power to obtain the resources of the earth for the advancement of the Kingdom of God (Gen. 1:26-29; Deut. 8:18; Matt. 6:33; 2 Cor. 8:9; 9:8; Phil. 4:19). Furthermore, it is our inheritance to walk in divine health (Ex. 15:26; 23:25-26; Deut. 7:15; Is. 53:5; Matt. 8:16-17; 1 Peter 2:24; 3 Jn. 1:2); and it is our inheritance to walk in victory (1 Cor. 15:57; 2 Cor. 2:14; 1 Jn. 5:4-6).

Now concerning our inheritance to be realised in the future life of the Millennial age and eternal state of the righteous – firstly, our future inheritance is that God has prepared immortal bodies for the saints to inherit the Kingdom of God (1 Cor. 15:35-55; 2 Cor. 5:1-5; Phil. 3;20-21). Secondly, in the Millennial reign of Christ, the glorified saints will reign with Him and rule the nations of the earth with a rod of iron (Ps. 2:7-9; Rev. 2:26-27; 5;9-10; 20:4-6). Thirdly, the saints of the Most High shall judge the world and angels (1 Cor. 6:1-3). Fourthly, the saints shall inherit and live with God and Christ in the New Jerusalem (Rev. 21-22). Lastly, there will be an eternal and visibly realised fellowship with the Father and the Son, the essential core of eternal life (Jn. 17:3; 1 Jn. 1:3; 3:1-3; Matt. 5:8; Heb. 12:14; Rev. 22:4). All these are glorious benefits awaiting the consummation of all things. What an awesome time that will be and all those who have this hope purify themselves even as he is pure (1 Jn. 3:3).

However, in the meantime, we must suffer, endure and overcome temptations, trials and persecutions to be accounted worthy to inherit the Kingdom of God. The Bible confirms this in Acts,

""Confirming the souls of the disciples, and exhorting them to continue in the faith, and that we must through much tribulation enter into the kingdom of God" (Acts. 14:22).

Tribulation is the necessary pathway into the glorious inheritance of the Kingdom of God. As joint-heirs with Christ, we not only inherit what He inherited, we also suffer as He suffered. He had to first suffer and then enter into His glory (Lk. 24:26; 1 Peter 1:10-11). It is mandatory to take the good with the bad. Everyone who has ceased to live in sin and to walk in righteousness will come against the ideologies, practices and values of the world that are antithetical to the values of the Kingdom of God, of which, you are a representative. The Apostle Peter exclaims,

"Forasmuch then as Christ hath suffered for us in the flesh, arm yourselves likewise with the same mind: for he that hath suffered in the flesh hath ceased from sin" (1 Peter 4:1).

Tribulations, persecutions and sufferings are the result of one's resistance and fight against sin, the flesh, the Devil and the world (Heb. 12:4). If you are experiencing no persecution or trial in your Christian walk, it is because you have compromised the truth of God's Word, but those who live godly will suffer persecution (2 Tim. 3:12) and those who suffer with Him shall reign with Him (2 Tim. 2:12).

The Revelation of the Glory of God in the Saints

The Apostle Paul was eminently qualified to speak as he did due to the fact that he suffered much for the furtherance of the Gospel (2 Cor. 11). He declared,

"...that the sufferings of this present time are not worthy to be compared with the glory which shall be revealed in us" (v18).

In this verse the apostle has considered and concluded that the sufferings of this present time is nothing in value to be compared with the glory which shall be revealed in us. There is no comparison in value or quantity. The glory of the New Covenant, of which we are a part, far exceeds the Old Covenant (2 Cor. 3), as are the sufferings of this age, whether for the Gospel of Jesus Christ or as part of the universal curse that came about by sin (Rom. 5:12). The Apostle said it like this:

"For our light affliction, which is but for a moment, worketh for us a far more exceeding and eternal weight of glory" (2 Cor. 4:17).

This verse reiterates what I just said; the glory of God in us is weighty and eternal in value and quantity in contrast to our afflictions which are light in value, and momentary. Afflictions, sufferings and persecutions are light in weight in comparison to the glory that shall be revealed in us. When the future glory shall be revealed, we will realise that we have not suffered enough. It is obvious to recognise with a spiritual mind that what God accomplished in Christ far exceeds what Satan achieved in Adam. The Word of God exclaims,

"Moreover the law entered that the offence might abound. But where sin abounded, grace did much more abound: That as sin hath reigned unto death, even so might grace reign through righteousness unto eternal life by Jesus Christ our Lord" (Rom. 5:20-21).

As sin was abundant in measure, God's grace was much more abounding in measure going beyond what is ordinary and necessary. So when the Bible mentions us being the righteousness of God in Christ (2 Cor. 6:21), we are not merely righteous; we are infinitely righteous because our righteousness originates from God: the infinite One. The price of the sacrifice of God's Son was infinite in value (Acts 20:28).

When our minds are focused on the glory that resides in us, we will possess tremendous power to endure the sufferings and trials that come against us because the current sufferings we go through will be eclipsed by the exceeding greatness of His glory. And that is why the Apostle Paul says,

"While we look not at the things which are seen, but at the things which are not seen: for the things which are seen are temporal; but the things not seen are eternal" (2 Cor. 4:18).

The invisible things that pertain to the glory of God have not been revealed yet can only be perceived through faith, for faith is the eye of the recreated human spirit, and the spiritual sense of sight is nurtured and exercised by prayer and the ministry of the Word of God (Jer. 33:3; 2 Cor. 3:18). As we do these things on a daily basis, though the outward man perish, the inward man will be renewed day by day. Any sufferings for righteousness sake or for the sake of the Gospel will not be in vain. There is a reward awaiting us in heaven that will far exceed the trials of this present life.

9

The Manifestation of the Sons of God

"For the earnest expectation of the creature waiteth for the manifestation of the sons of God. For the creature was made subject to vanity, not willingly, but by reason of him who hath subjected the same in hope, Because the creature itself also shall be delivered from the bondage of corruption into the glorious liberty of the children of God. For we know that the whole creation groaneth and travaileth in pain together until now" (Rom. 8:19-22).

Paul's train of thought is continued and developed in verse 19 of the opening passage concerning the glory which shall be revealed in us (v18). The Greek noun for "manifestation" is akin to the Greek verb for "revealed". Its noun is "apokalupsis", meaning revelation, and it signifies the removing of the veil or covering. So the verse is actually saying that creation is earnestly awaiting the revelation or unveiling of the sons of God as a result of the glory being revealed in them. Creation is intensely and expectedly yearning for the revelation of the sons of God. That time will fully come when our mortal veil, that is our flesh, will be removed so that the glory of God in us will shine to this groaning creation (1 Cor. 15:43; Phil. 3:21; Heb. 10:20).

Verse 20 tells us why the whole of creation is earnestly hoping for the believers' divine sonship to be revealed:

"For the creature was made subject to vanity, not willingly, but of reason of him who hath subjected the same in hope."

In the beginning of creation, as recorded in the book of Genesis, man sinned and brought death into God's creation (Gen. 3; Rom. 5:12). So God, by means of divine judgment, made His whole creation subject to vanity. The Greek rendering of vanity is "mataiotes" which is akin to "mataios", and it denotes emptiness as to results. Its adjective implies being void of results and is used for idolatrous practices (Acts 14:15); the thoughts of the wise (1 Cor. 3:20); faith if Christ is not risen from death (1 Cor. 15:17); foolish questions, genealogies and strife about the Law (Tit. 3:9); religion without a bridled tongue (Ja. 1:26); way of life (1 Peter 1:18); and creation itself (v20), which is our focus in this chapter.

Creation being made subject to vanity, according to the Greek meaning, became subject to the absence of practical aim, purpose, results and effect to which creation was originally and divinely designated. In God's creation before the fall, He saw everything to be very good (Gen. 1:4, 10, 12, 18, 21, 25, 31). It was free from everything that pertained to corruption, death, bondage and pain until the spiritual fall of man brought them into this world. And so creation in its present state is not functioning at its full potential in the way it was designed because of the presence of the curse.

Now the creation that the apostle refers to is first of all distinguished from believers according to verse 23 which says, "And not only they (referring to creation), but ourselves also…" Furthermore, in verses 19 and 21, creation is mentioned distinctly from the sons of God and the children of God. Also, creation itself excludes fallen and unregenerate humanity, for sinners are not earnestly expecting or desiring to see the manifestation of the sons of God which will be concurrent with the second advent known as the revelation or appearing of Jesus Christ (1 Peter 1:7, 13; Tit. 2:13; 1 Jn. 3:2-3; Col. 3:4). On the contrary, their response will be one of fear and mourning (Matt. 24:30; Rev. 1:7; 6:12-17). Therefore, by deductive reasoning, the option left is that creation alludes to the natural vegetation, animal life and inanimate things, the weather conditions, the topography of the earth, seas, lakes and rivers that have been affected by the curse.

In verse 21, the future hope and expectation of creation itself is that it shall be delivered from the bondage of corruption into the glorious liberty of the children of God. Creation itself partook of the consequences of Adam's sin. The earth was cursed for man's sake; thorns and thistles growing from the ground as reminded emblems of the earth's cursed state (Gen. 2:17-18; 5;29). Cain's hatred and murderous act against his brother caused the earth not to yield her strength to him (Gen. 4:8-12). In certain parts of the earth, lands have suffered famine and droughts with the destruction of vegetation; animals have been struck with deadly diseases and starvation, mildew, floods and natural disasters due to adverse weather conditions. Earthquakes, floods and volcanic eruptions have changed the topography of lands, destroying livelihoods. From the beginning of creation until now, many species of animals have been extinct. Prior to the Adamic Fall and the Flood of Noah, all animal life was herbivorous, including man (Gen. 1:29-30). After the Flood, some species of animal life became carnivorous, while others became dangerous, venomous and aggressive. Nature spiralled into disharmony and belligerence (Gen. 9:1-5). All that I have mentioned in creation and nature regarding their present hostility, frailty and deterioration are what the apostle calls "the bondage of corruption." He also describes the whole creation in verse 22:

"For we know that the whole creation groaneth and travaileth in pain together until now."

There are two key words I want to look at in this verse: "groaneth" and "travaileth." The former is translated from the Greek word "stenazo", and it defines groaning to be of an inward, unexpressed feeling of sorrow and is translated as "with grief" (Heb. 13:17); "sighed" (Mk. 7:34); "groan" (Rom. 8:23; 2 Cor. 5:2, 4); and "grudge" (Ja. 5:9). The latter word "travaileth" is from the Greek rendering "sunodino", signifying "birth pangs", and is used of inevitable destruction coming upon the ungodly at the Day of the Lord (1 Thess. 5:3); of the Apostle's labour in the gospel to have Christ formed in them (Gal. 4:19); and of catastrophies and disasters - signs of Christ's Second Coming (Matt. 24:8). So joining both definitions, the meaning is that the whole creation together groans with unexpressed feelings of sorrow, and birth pangs of natural disasters and catastrophes such as famines, pestilence, earthquakes, violent storms and weather patterns – floods, tornados and tsunamis. They are signs of creation travailing of which Jesus predicted will become more frequent and intense as we approach His Second Coming - the time for the manifestation of the sons of God (Matt. 24:1-8).

When that time shall come for the sons of God to be manifested, the whole creation will be delivered from the bondage of corruption it was under since the fall of man, into the glorious liberty of the children of God (Rom. 8:19, 21). The Old Testament prophets give a vivid description of what that is going to be like (Acts 3:21).

"The wolf also shall dwell with the lamb, and the leopard shall lie down with the kid; and the calf and the young lion and the fatling together; and a little child shall lead them. And the cow and the bear shall feed; their young ones shall lie down together: and the lion shall eat straw like the ox. And the suckling child shall play on the hole of the asp, and the weaned child shall put his hand on the cockatrice' den. They shall not hurt or destroy in all my holy mountain: for the earth shall be full of the knowledge of the LORD, as the waters cover the sea" (Is. 11:6-9; see also Is. 65:25).

Here, the Prophet Isaiah describes the restoration of the animal kingdom to what it was before sin entered the world. There is harmony and peace between livestock and predators, herbivores and carnivors. The carnivorous nature of the lion, the leopard and the bear will be taken from them and they shall become herbivorous as it was prior to the Flood. And children will no more be harmed by serpents. Dominion will be restored to humanity, for a little child shall lead them (Gen. 1:26-28). Righteousness, harmony and peace will pervade the whole creation because the knowledge of the LORD will fill the whole earth as the waters cover the sea (vii). This is also proclaimed in other passages of the Old Testament:

"But as truly as I live, all the earth shall be filled with the glory of the LORD...For the earth shall be filled with the knowledge of the glory of the LORD, as the waters cover the sea" (Num. 14:21; Hab. 2:14).

The knowledge of the glory of God will bring about peace and harmony in creation as spoken by the Prophet Isaiah; that glory is literally termed in the Greek by the Apostle Paul as "the liberty of the glory of the children of God" (Rom. 8:21). This knowledge of the glory of God is a treasure that is resident in our earthen vessels according to 2 Corinthians 4:6-7:

"For God, who commanded the light to shine out of darkness, hath shined in our hearts, to give the light of the knowledge of the glory of God in the face of Jesus Christ. But we have this treasure in earthen vessels, that the excellency of the power may be of God and not of us."

Creation is earnestly expecting the knowledge of this glory resident in you to be revealed to the world at the Second Coming of Jesus Christ. However, we do not need to wait for His Second Coming for it to be revealed. We are experiencing a foretaste of its revelation and power now (Heb. 6:5). The nature of that glory is liberty and when we came in contact with that glory, we were set free from the bondage of sin. Now we have the responsibility to manifest that glorious liberty to the world by exercising our dominion as sons of God over sin, sickness, disease and devils. Jesus showed forth His glory by setting the captives free from the oppression of the Devil (Matt. 8:16-17; Acts 10:38; 1 Jn. 3:8). Let us practise manifesting ourselves as sons of God now before we are manifested as sons in the world to come.

In the revelation of the glory of God in the world to come, joy and gladness will be expressed through the nation of Israel, the topography and natural vegetation of the earth as described by the Prophet Isaiah,

"For ye shall go out with joy, and be led forth with peace: the mountains and the hills shall break forth before you into singing, and all the trees of the field shall clap their hands. Instead of the thorn shall come up the fir tree, and instead of the brier shall come up the myrtle tree..." (Is. 55:12-13).

The manifestation of the sons of God will cause Israel to go out in joy and be led forth with peace. Peace and joy will be so abundant that they will cascade into the atmosphere and the whole creation that the poetic expression is that the mountains and hills will sing and the trees of the field shall clap their hands. Allow the knowledge of the glory of God to shine out of you so that it brings joy and peace to people's lives instead of weeping, and blessings instead of a curse – emblematic of thorns and briers.

I am reminded of a woman, who attended my church, who was suffering from peptic ulcers; she had not eaten anything that morning. She came forward for prayer. She told me her problem. Then I exercised my sonship authority in Christ, who said that if I laid hands on the sick, they would recover (Mk. 16:17). I commanded the peptic ulcers to go and the pain to leave; she was instantly set free from the condition. We are called to deliver the sick, the afflicted, the oppressed and the prisoners out of the bondage of corruption into the glorious liberty of the children of God (Rom. 8:19).

10

The Firstfruits of the Spirit

"And not only they, but ourselves also, which have the firstfruits of the Spirit, even we ourselves groan within ourselves, waiting for the adoption, to wit, the redemption of the body" (Rom. 8:23).

This opening passage of scripture must be seen in the light of the subject and context discussed by the apostle, namely, the glorious manifestation of the sons of God liberating the whole creation from the bondage of corruption (v19-22). As creation earnestly expects and groans while awaiting its liberation by the revelation of God's sons, the apostle adds that we, as Christian believers, are also groaning within ourselves because we are earnestly expecting and awaiting the future adoption which is the redemption of our bodies. And the very thing given as security of that fact is the Holy Spirit. This forms the essence of my discussion in this chapter.

At the root of a true Christian believer, his heart is groaning, yearning, mourning and passionately expecting the glorious appearing of our Lord and Saviour: Jesus Christ – a hope that saturates his being while not visibly realised as yet. Consequently, in the meantime, he lives with a deep sigh and unexpressed groaning of sorrow that is awaiting his appointed time of change. It is of this that our Lord inferred in His teachings on the Beatitudes:

"Blessed are they that mourn: for they shall be comforted" (Matt. 5:4).

This mourning is after a godly sort that leads to true comfort, but the sorrow of the world works death (2 Cor. 7:9-10). Godly sorrow has a threefold purpose: 1) it leads to repentance (2 Cor. 7:10); 2) it engages in godly intercession for the sins and sufferings of the world; 3) it earnestly desires and yearns for His soon return and the moment of change for every believer (Rom. 8:15; 2 Cor. 5:2, 4). That change is referring to a transformation of bodies. The apostle Paul alludes to this by saying,

"For we know that if our earthly house of this tabernacle were dissolved, we have a building of God, an house not made with hands, eternal in the heavens. For in this we groan, earnestly desiring to be clothed upon with our house which is from heaven...For we that are in this tabernacle do groan, being burdened: not for that we would be unclothed, but clothed upon, that mortality might be swallowed up of life. Now he that hath wrought us for the selfsame thing is God, who also hath given unto us the earnest of the Spirit" (2 Cor. 5:1-2, 4-5).

Paul describes the thing that we are earnestly yearning to transpire. This groaning or unexpressed feeling of sorrow arises from its deep rooted desire to be clothed upon with immortality (v2, 4). The Greek term for "groan" is the same word used in

Romans 8:23, the object of which is the adoption: the redemption of the body. In the above passage of scripture, the apostle explains what the redemption of the body is: - a change from the earthly house of this tabernacle to a building of God, eternal in the heavens that can never be destroyed (2 Cor. 5:1).

The earthly house of this tabernacle is used by the apostle to convey some important truths about our mortal bodies in which we dwell on the earth. The Greek term is "skenos", which means a tent as a dwelling place for the "nephesh" – the soul, the person, or the life. For example, Abraham, Isaac and Jacob dwelt in tents (Heb. 11:9), and afterwards the children of Israel did the same during their wilderness wanderings (Ex. 16:16). Furthermore, there was a tent of meeting where the Presence of the Lord dwelt, situated in the centre of the camp of Israel (Acts 7:44; Heb. 8:5; 9:1). These tabernacles were types and shadows of a spiritual truth (Heb. 10:1; Col. 2:17).

As a tabernacle was a fragile and weak structure, the physical body is weak and transient in contrast to the spiritual body which is strong, robust and eternal. Our earthly existence in our mortal bodies is only for a short time. Our physical bodies, defined as tabernacles, testify to the fact that we are strangers, pilgrims and sojourners on the earth, like Abraham, looking for that Heavenly City that has foundations whose builder and maker is God (Heb. 11:9-10, 13, 16). A tent was not a permanent structure; it was mobile, and therefore, was used by those who were on a journey travelling to their destination. Heaven is our destination and celestial home, not earth (1 Peter 1:17; 2:11).

Then our physical body is the dwelling place of our soul: the unseen personality – the real you. Your physical body is not all there is of you; the Word of God describes the real you as the inward man or hidden man of the heart (2 Cor. 4:16; 1 Peter 3:4). That is why if you die, the real you will continue to exist. In death, you depart from the body of this tabernacle to be present with the Lord. This is the manner in which the apostle describes it,

"We are confident, I say, and willing rather to be absent from the body and to be present with the Lord" (2 Cor. 5:8).

In the future, there is going to be exchange of bodies, the spiritual, celestial body for the natural, earthly body. As we have borne the image of the earthy, we shall also bear the image of the heavenly (1 Cor. 15:49. It is a building of God reserved for us in heaven (2 Cor. 5:1-4).

God has given us something to remind us of our future inheritance: the fullness of our redemption. In the opening scripture to this chapter, it declares,

"And not only they, but ourselves also, which have the firstfruits of the Spirit..." (Rom. 8:23a).

Now we come to the main theme of this chapter: God has given unto us the firstfruits of the Spirit. What that denotes is that we have been given the Holy Spirit Himself who is the firstfruits. Let us examine its terminology and meaning in detail. The Greek word for "firstfruits" is "aparche", which signifies the earliest ripening period of the crops prior to its full harvest, or the first ripening of a tree preceding its full produce. This portion of harvest was dedicated to God as a representation of the full harvest that was to come (Ex. 23:16). It served as a guarantee of the imminent arrival of the whole harvest; hence, Christ is called the firstfruits of them that slept – His resurrection is a guarantee of the future resurrection of all believers (1 Cor. 15:20, 23). And so, the receiving of the Holy Spirit also serves as a guarantee of our full redemption.

Firstfruits of the Spirit alludes to the outpouring of the Spirit on the Day of Pentecost because that was the day when the two loaves of bread made from the firstfruits of the wheat harvest was presented to God (Lev. 23:16-17). That day was known as "the Day of the Firstfruits" (Num. 28:26). It was also called "the Feast of Weeks, of the firstfruits of wheat harvest" (Ex. 34:22). In Exodus 23:16, it was designated "the Feast of Harvest, of the firstfruits of thy labours." So when the Apostle Paul speaks of the firstfruits of the Spirit, he is referring to the baptism in the Holy Spirit, an experience that commenced on the Day of Pentecost. Therefore, this infilling of the Spirit marks the Early Churches empowerment (Acts 1:8; 2:1-4).

An equivalent terminology, used in the New Testament, to convey this truth, is "earnest of the Spirit" (2 Cor. 5:5). The Greek rendering for "earnest" is "arrabon", which originally signified earnest-money deposited by the purchaser as an assurance that the full payment would be made at a later date, and if not, the purchase was forfeited. In its general usage, it came to mean an earnest or pledge of any sort. The word is used of the Holy Spirit to be a Divine earnest or pledge of all our future blessedness (2 Cor. 1:22; 5:5; Eph. 1:13). According to the context of 2 Corinthians 5:5, the earnest of the Spirit is a deposit and a guarantee of our full inheritance which commences with the change of our earthly bodies to spiritual, celestial bodies: - the earthly house of this tabernacle, to a building from heaven (2 Cor. 5:1-5).

There is a word that is used in connection with the term "earnest" in three passages of scripture:

"Now he which stablisheth you with us in Christ, and hath anointed us, is God; Who hath also sealed us, and given the earnest of the Spirit in our hearts...In whom ye also trusted, after that ye heard the word of truth, the gospel of your salvation: in whom also after that ye believed, ye were sealed with that Holy Spirit of promise, Which is the earnest of our inheritance until the redemption of the purchased possession, unto the praise of his glory...And grieve not the Holy Spirit of God, whereby ye are sealed unto the day of redemption" (2 Cor. 1:21-22; Eph. 1:13-14; 4:30).

That term referred to above, is the word, "sealed." So the Holy Spirit is the Firstfruits, the earnest and the Seal of our full redemptive inheritance. The Greek word for "sealed" is "sphragizo", akin to its noun: "sphragis", denoting a seal or signet. A seal was used as an emblem of ownership. In 2 Timothy 2:19, it states,

"Nevertheless the foundation of God standeth sure, having this seal. The Lord knoweth them that are his..."

In the Book of Revelation, the 144, 000 Jews were sealed with the seal of the living God, authenticating them to be the servants of the living God (7:2-8). Likewise, the baptism in the Holy Spirit confirms and authenticates those who truly belong to God. The Presence of God by His Spirit in His people is emblematic of His ownership of them. Romans 8:9b intimates,

The Firstfruits of the Spirit

"...Now if any man have not the Spirit of Christ, he is none of his."

As God dwelling in the midst of His people bore evidence that Israel was His people, so God's Spirit in New Covenant believers testify to His ownership of them. The Scripture states,

"What? Know ye not that your body is the temple of the Holy Ghost which is in you, which ye have of God, and ye are not your own? For ye are bought with a price: therefore glorify God in your body, and in your spirit, which are God's" (1 Cor. 6:19-20).

Jesus Christ, our Lord and Master, has bought us with the price of His own blood and the baptism in the Holy Spirit is a seal or sign of ownership. When the Holy Spirit was poured out upon the Gentiles, it testified to the Jewish believers that God had granted the Gentiles repentance unto life (Acts 10:44-48; 11:14-18). In the new birth, you become Christ's and by the baptism in the Holy Spirit, you are sealed after you believed the truth: the gospel of your salvation (Eph. 1:13).

A seal in Bible times also signified security. The seal of the Holy Spirit is a pledge that secures the fulfilment of a promise. Ephesians 1:13-14 and 4:30 states,

"...ye were sealed with that Holy Spirit of promise, which is the earnest [pledge] of our inheritance until the redemption of the purchase possession...And grieve not the Holy Spirit of God, whereby ye are sealed unto the day of redemption."

The seal of the Holy Spirit secures you for your future and destiny. That destiny is the day of redemption or the redemption of the purchased possession. If you are born again – redeemed by the blood of Jesus Christ - you are now God's purchased possession and the time is coming when you will enter into your full inheritance (1 Cor. 15:30) by the redemption of your body at the Second Coming of Christ (Rom. 8:23). The Holy Spirit bears witness and empowers us to endure unto our future destiny of redemption, blessings, inheritance and adoption. He is the seal of our eternal security (Jn. 10:28-29).

In the biblical teaching of adoption in the New Testament, there are two aspects to our adoption: a past and a future aspect. With regard to the redemptive work of Christ, we were made sons as a result of His sacrificial work on the Cross, according to Galatians 4:4-7. We are now sons and not slaves. But in the future aspect of our adoption, our bodies shall be redeemed from corruption to inherit incorruption. In 1 Corinthians 13:9-13 the Apostle Paul compares this transition from mortality to immortality, the imperfect to the perfect age under the imagery of his growth from childhood to adulthood, as the culture of adoption is described in Galatians 4:1-5. The culmination of our adoption as sons shall be manifested in glory to the world at the appointed time: Christ's Second Coming (Rom. 8:19-23; 1Jn. 3:1-3). But in the meantime, we see through a glass darkly for we know in part and prophesy in part (1 Cor. 13:9, 12). And for this reason God has anointed us with the firstfruits of His Spirit as a deposit of our full redemption. While we have this hope, let us purify ourselves as He is pure (1 Jn. 3:3).

11

Saved by Hope

"For we are saved by hope: but hope that is seen is not hope: for what a man seeth, why doth he yet hope for? But if we hope for that we see not, then do we with patience wait for it" (Rom. 8:24-25).

While faith is the evidence of unseen realities, hope is the earnest expectation of their future, visible realisation (Heb. 11:1). As faith seizes the promise in the present, hope expects its manifestation in the future (Mk. 11:24). Faith and hope are inseparably related in the biblical definition of faith:

"Now faith is the substance of things hoped for, the evidence of things not seen" (Heb. 11:1).

Hope is the object of faith: it is the thing that faith seeks to accomplish. Hope is like a thermostat that sets the temperature for the power in the boiler or the radiator to achieve. Without hope, there would be nothing for the substance of faith to work towards. In actual fact, if there is no hope, there is no faith, for faith is the substance of things hoped for. Hope is the blueprint of what your faith desires to accomplish. A blueprint is a plan, a design or picture of something that is desired to become physical reality. In architecture, when a house or building is requested to be built, you begin first with a schematic drawing of how you desire your house or building to look. Once that design is drawn up, you then need to employ a skilled workforce to build according to the blueprint. In like manner, your faith is the workforce that you employ to accomplish the desired results according to your vision or planned expectation called hope, resident in your heart.

When something you hope for becomes a visible reality, it ceases to be hope, for hope that is seen is no longer hope (Rom. 8:24-25). Like faith, hope is something that cannot be seen or touched by the natural senses. It remains an expectation until the future becomes a present, visible realisation.

Now if faith and hope have an inseparable relationship, if we are saved by faith (Eph. 2:8), then we are also saved by hope (Rom. 8:24). We began our Christian walk by faith in Jesus Christ, our Lord and Saviour, and were therefore saved from our sins. However, to maintain that salvation in the midst of persecution, temptation and affliction are going to take hope. That hope looks forwards and expectedly to the future realisation and glorious return of Jesus Christ and the full manifestation of our inheritance. This hope sustains and empowers your faith to endure and persevere to the end. While our faith focuses on the present, our hope focuses on the future. Hebrews 6:18-19 states,

"That by two immutable things, in which it was impossible to lie, we might have a strong consolation, who have fled for refuge to lay hold upon the hope SET BEFORE US: Which hope we have as an anchor of the soul, both sure and steadfast, and which entereth into that within the veil."

The Hebrew writer describes hope as an anchor of the soul, both sure and steadfast - a hope that is set before us. The future hope set before us anchors our soul and prevents us from wavering, but keeps us steadfast. An anchor is designed to keep a boat or ship from drifting away from the seashore. It is the wavering seas and the winds that cause instability for a ship without an anchor. To doubt is to be like the wavering seas and to be driven by every wind of doctrine (Ja. 1:6; Eph. 4:14). Hope gives us a strong consolation that is sure and steadfast; a refuge against the very storms and challenges of life. Without it, you will become weak and fall under the weight of your challenges. Proverbs 13:12 teaches us,

"Hope deferred makes the heart sick: but when the desire cometh, it is a tree of life."

When you lose hope, your heart becomes weak and sickly; your attitude and perception of life experiences despondency, discouragement, fear and depression, sometimes culminating in suicidal thoughts. As a result, people end up taking their lives or being admitted to a mental hospital because of suffering a nervous breakdown due to the fact that their heart was weak. Proverbs 24:10 states,

"If thou faint in the day of adversity, thy strength is small."

If a person's strength is small, how do you develop it? You develop what is known as endurance strength through the power of hope. There are two aspects to how one possesses hope: 1) the

Scriptures (Rom. 15:4; 2) putting hope to work (Rom. 5:3-4).

The Scriptures

"For whatsoever things were written aforetime were written for our learning, that we through patience and comfort of the scriptures might have hope" (Rom. 15:4).

This verse confirms that the key to walking in Bible hope is to learn the Scriptures for they were written for this purpose: that you may learn and have hope. And in having hope, you will have comfort of the scriptures and patience to keep standing. The Greek term for "patience" is "hupomones", meaning endurance and the Greek word literally means to abide or remain under. It is the idea of resisting the very thing that you are abiding under.

The Greek rendering for "learning" in the above passage of scripture is "didaskalia", and it denotes teaching or instruction. Giving oneself to the study of God's Word is tantamount to giving attendance to teaching and instruction. Without the Word of God, you cannot possess hope, for hope comes by the Word of God in the same manner that faith comes by the Word (Rom. 10:17). If you do not give quality time and attention to God's instruction and teaching in His Word, you will not have the hope to comfort and sustain you in times of trials and suffering, for in those times, the Word you have deposited in you will comfort, teach, instruct and strengthen you. What you do not put in will not come out when you need it. So in times when your back is not against the wall, build yourself up in the Word (Acts 20:32) and you will have all the endurance strength you need to stand.

Putting Hope to Work

"And not only so, but we glory in tribulations also: knowing that tribulation worketh patience; And patience, experience; and experience, hope" (Rom. 5:3-4).

Paul informs us in verse 2 of chapter 5 that we rejoice in hope of the glory of God. This is the glory that is to be revealed in us – the glory of the liberty of the children of God - that the apostle spoke about in verses 18 and 21. At present, that glory has not been revealed or seen as yet. While it is not seen, it is hope - the joyful expectation of something good. This is why the apostle calls it the hope of the glory of God. And because of that joyful expectation, we can also rejoice or glory in tribulations. Having the joyful expectation prepares and strengthens us for tribulations. The Bible does teach us that the joy of the Lord is our strength (Neh. 8:10).

The Greek rendering of "tribulation" is "thlipsis", and it denotes a pressing or the application of pressure by adverse circumstances; hence, it signifies to suffer affliction or trouble. When pressure is applied because of circumstances, we do not glory because of them but in them; we rejoice expectantly for the revelation of the glory of God which fuels us with endurance-strength.

Tribulation employs a trichotomy of things to work in our favour. Paul lists them as patience, experience and hope. It is important to note that faith does not come by tribulation, it comes by the Word of God (Rom. 10:17). The reason why tribulation comes is stated in Mark 4:16-17,

"These are they likewise which are sown on stony ground; who, when they have heard the word, immediately receive it with gladness; And have no root in themselves, and so endure but for a time: afterward, when affliction [Gk thlipsis; tribulation] or persecution ariseth for the word's sake, immediately they are offended."

Tribulation arises for the Word's sake. That is when you hear and gladly receive the Word, the enemy brings tribulation or persecution to cause you to become offended. The Greek term "offended" here is "skandalizo", which means to put a snare or stumbling block in the way to cause someone to be entrapped or stumble, so as to fall. The ethical idea is to be hindered from walking the faith-walk or stumble, in order to fall from one's spiritual and moral stance. The Devil does not want the Word to be deeply rooted in you, so he sends affliction or persecution to stop that Word from penetrating deeply into the soil of your heart, because once it does, it will be extremely difficult to root it out, so he tries to get you offended at the early stages of revelation. Hebrews 10:32 states,

"but call to remembrance the former days, in which, after ye were illuminated, ye endured a great fight of affliction."

So tribulation does not minister faith and hope; to the contrary, it seeks to destroy your faith and hope by removing their source: the Word of God (Rom. 10:17; 15:4).

When the recipient of the Word is determined to stand and persevere on its promises, then tribulation puts to work in him, endurance, which is spiritual and moral resistance to the pressures it is bringing.

Then patient endurance puts to work experience. That word "experience" in the Greek rendering is "dokime", and it implies the process of proving; the proving of you. In addition, it denotes the result of proving or testing. Hence, endurance and perseverance put to work the process of testing to determine whether you are approved of God and counted worthy to enter His eternal Kingdom. The Bible teaches that we must, through much tribulation, enter the Kingdom of God (Acts 14:22). It is necessary and inevitable that you will be tested and proved, prior to spiritual promotion. God will prove His people; this is how He deals with those who are called to inherit His Kingdom to see if they will meet His approval. The Lord testing his called-out ones is replete in Scripture. Joseph (Ps. 105:17-19); Abraham (Gen. 22); the children of Israel (Deut. 8); and even our Lord and Saviour Jesus Christ was tested (Matt. 4; Heb. 4:15; 5:9). Therefore, let us prepare our hearts to be proved in the fires of affliction so that we may be found worthy to enter into His glory.

Lastly, the process of proving puts to work, hope. For hope to work on our behalf, it must already be in us so that when trials, temptations and persecution arise, hope will anchor our souls to be steadfast, consistent and immovable in adverse times. It will actually save us from making shipwreck of our faith. Hope will help and sustain us in our times of infirmities (Heb. 4:15).

12

Holy Spirit Intercession

"Likewise the Spirit also helpeth our infirmities: for we know not what we should pray for as we ought: but the Spirit itself maketh intercession for us with groanings which cannot be uttered. And he that searcheth the hearts knoweth what is the mind of the Spirit, because he maketh intercession for the saints according to the will of God" (Rom. 8:26-27).

Holy Spirit intercession forms part of His role and ministry towards believers as their Paraclete. This title stems from the Greek rendering: "parakletos", which literally means "one called alongside to help." The word is translated in the King James Bible as comforter (Jn. 14:16, 26; 15:26; 16:7) and advocate (1 Jn. 21). It is used once of Christ and four times of the Holy Spirit. There are other synonyms that convey the ministry of the Paraclete – the Holy Spirit. They are helper, strengthener, standby, counsellor and intercessor. It is the intercessory aspect of the ministry of the Holy Spirit that I want to deal with in this chapter.

In the above scriptural passage, there are three important aspects to the intercessory ministry of the Holy Spirit in the believer:

1) He helps us in our weaknesses
2) He makes intercession for us
3) He makes intercession according to the will of God

The scriptural passage begins by saying: "Likewise the Spirit helpeth our infirmities..." The term "likewise" connects this verse (v26) with the previous topic about being saved by hope. In other words, there is a similarity between the Holy Spirit's ministry and the function of hope in the believer; and that similarity is this: as hope helps, strengthens and sustains the believer in his infirmities, so does the Holy Spirit helps, strengthens, bolsters and sustains the believer in his weaknesses. The mode of help may be different from the method of hope, but the accomplishing effect is the same.

The verb "helpeth" informs us of the subject of the sentence: the Holy Spirit, does. Its Greek expression is "sunantilambano", and it signifies to take hold together with. Vine (1984:214) defines this word as,

"...to take hold with at the side for assistance...; hence to take a share in, help in bearing, help in general...it is used...in Martha's request to the Lord to bid her sister help her, Luke 10:40..."

This explanation and example simply show us what the Spirit does in the life of a believer. Firstly, it unveils what He does not do: He does not merely do the work instead of the believer. Secondly, the Greek word shows us that the Spirit's role is to do the work with the believer, so neither does the work exclusively or alone. The Holy Spirit assists us in our infirmities or weaknesses through the ministry of intercessory prayer, thus alleviating or removing the burdens together with Him.

The infirmities with which the Spirit will help us are human weaknesses. Those weaknesses are as follows: ignorance about what to pray for (Rom. 8:26); temptations, trials and sufferings (2 Cor. 12:9-10; Heb. 4:15); moral weakness of the flesh (Rom. 6:19; Heb. 7:27-28). These are the specific weaknesses for which the Holy Spirit will help you. And the way the Spirit will assist you is through His intercession in you – the believer.

The primary human weakness focused on in verse 26 is that we do not know what to pray for as we ought, but the Spirit Himself makes intercession for us. This is how He helps us. When we do not know what to pray for, the Holy Spirit assists us in prayer. How does He help us? By making intercession. This intercessory prayer is done by the Spirit Himself within us. The Spirit intercedes through us. That Spirit intercession is performed with groanings which cannot be uttered.

The clause "groanings which cannot be uttered" is translated from the Greek words "stenagmois alaletois", which signify unutterable groans or sighs that we fail to put into words or articulate speech. They are unutterable groans because we do not know what to pray as we should. It is an infirmity or weakness of not being able to put those inexpressible groanings into words. This is where the Holy Spirt comes in to help – to take hold together with you, those deep-seated groans and express them in articulate speech. This is accomplished by you yielding your tongue to the Spirit, and the Spirit interceding by giving you a language with which to articulate those unutterable groanings to God. Hence the Spirit Himself makes intercession for us. According to the New Testament revelation, the Spirit gives us a prayer language with which to express ourselves to God and it is called "speaking in tongues". It is defined as speaking supernaturally by the Holy Spirit, a true language unlearned by the speaker. This phenomenon of tongues was first experienced by the 120 disciples in the upper room on the Day of Pentecost. Luke, the writer of the book of Acts, records this supernatural event, showing the divine and human responsibilities and their participation in this supernatural experience,

"And when the day of Pentecost was fully come, they were all with one accord in one place. And suddenly there came a sound from heaven, as of a rushing mighty wind, and it filled all the house where they were sitting. And there appeared unto them cloven tongues like as of fire, and it sat upon each of them. And they were all filled with the Holy Ghost, and began to speak with other tongues, as the Spirit gave them utterance" (Acts 2:1-4).

In this passage of scripture, it clearly informs us that when they were filled with the Holy Spirit, the 120 speak supernaturally true languages while the Spirit gave them utterance. It is the Spirit who gave the utterance while they did the speaking; an example of how the Spirit helps or takes hold together with us in our unutterable groanings, sighs and weaknesses because of not knowing what to pray (Rom. 8:26). But the Spirit lays hold of those unuttered groanings and articulate them through us and for us in intercession which does not involve our understanding or mental comprehension, so that our minds cease to be a hindrance to our communication with God. The Scripture states,

"For he that speaketh in an unknown tongue speaketh not unto men, but unto God; for no man understandeth him; howbeit in the spirit he speaketh mysteries. For if I pray in an unknown tongue, my spirit prayeth, but my understanding is unfruitful" (1 Cor. 14:2, 14).

When the Holy Spirit prays for you, He is also praying through your spirit. As He prays, your spirit also prays while your understanding remains unfruitful. Your spirit and the Holy Spirit are working together; hence the Greek term "sunantilambano" is chosen to depict what is happening with the intercession of the Spirit in the believer. That is why it is important for the Spirit-filled believer to give praying in the spirit precedence over praying with the intellect. The Apostle Paul capitulates to this view when he says,

"What is it then? I will pray with the spirit, and I will pray with the understanding also" (v15).

Praying in the spirit comes first and then praying with the understanding. In our own intellect, we do not always understand every thing that is going on in ourselves or our circumstances that we are praying about, and so praying in tongues activates the unlimited wisdom and knowledge of the Holy Spirit to intercede according to the perfect will of God. Verse 27 of Romans 8 declares,

"And he that searcheth the hearts knoweth what is the mind of the Spirit, because he maketh intercession for the saints according to the will of God."

The pronoun "he" is the subject of this verse, and is therefore a substitute for the name of the subject in the previous verse, and that name is the "Spirit". So the "he" of verse 27 is referring to the "Spirit" of verse 26. For example, if I said, "Peter went home from school. He had steak and potatoes for dinner." The "He" of the second sentence would be referring to Peter in the first sentence. In the same vein, the apostle is still dealing with the Holy Spirit as the subject of both verses (v26, 27). He that searches the hearts is alluding to the Spirit who is omniscient with regard to the hearts of men, and knows what is the mind of the Spirit.

In the original Greek language of the New Testament, the phrase "mind of the spirit" in verse 27 is also used by the apostle in verse 6 of the same chapter translated "to be spiritually minded." The passages relates to the mind of the regenerate spirit which is life and peace. Since the Spirit has within the scope of His knowledge the thoughts, the motives and intents of the heart, He also has knowledge of the thoughts, the intent and deep-seated motives of the recreated human spirit. This qualifies Him to intercede on our behalf, concerning things that we are unable to adequately express to God in words. Nevertheless, when we pray in the Spirit, we are endowed with the power of supernatural utterance to express ourselves to God in perfect harmony with His will.

The baptism in the Holy Spirit has a fourfold significance with regard to power: 1) we are clothed with supernatural power and ability (Lk. 24:49; Acts 1:8); 2) we are inspired with the power of utterance (Mk 16:17: Acts 1:8; 2:1-4, 16-18; 1 Cor. 14); 3) we are endowed with the power of insight (Jn. 14:26; 16:12-13; 1 Cor. 2:9-16; Eph. 1:16-19); and 4) we possess the power to perform supernatural signs and wonders (Mk. 16:17-20; Heb. 2:4; Jn. 14:12).

Here are the following benefits of Holy Spirit intercession:

1) it helps you to overcome human weaknesses (Rom. 8:26); a) ignorance - when praying in the Spirit, ignorance ceases to be a barrier to praying according to the will of God as was previously discussed in this chapter; b) praying in the Spirit strengthens you to overcome the weakness of temptation and persecution (Lk. 22:43, 46; Heb. 4:15; 2 Cor. 12:9-10); c) Spirit intercession helps you to overcome the moral weakness of human character (Rom. 6:19; Gal. 5:16); d) it will empower and give life to your human body (Rom. 8:11).

2) It is for personal edification: "He that speaketh in an unknown tongue edifieth himself..." (1 Cor. 14:4). The Greek term for "edify" is "oikodomeo", which literally means to build a house, but figuratively denotes spiritual development. The synonyms and phrases used to convey this concept are to grow, strengthen, embolden and increase. Most of my prayer time is spent praying in tongues because it is the most effective way of communicating with God. It is one hundred percent efficient, no time is wasted by reason of the fact that you are always praying according to the perfect will of God when you pray in the spirit. I would not have reached this far in God if I did not pray in tongues. By consequently praying in tongues, my understanding of the Word of God has developed drastically (see Jn. 16:12-13). Therefore, every believer must endeavour to be filled with the Spirit and to always make supplication in the Spirit (Eph. 6:18; Jude 1:20).

3) It is for spiritual rest and refreshing: "For with stammering lips and another tongue will he speak to this people.

To whom he said, This is the rest wherewith ye may cause the weary to rest; and this is the refreshing: yet they would not hear" (Is. 28:11-12). The Apostle Paul quotes this passage in His teaching on speaking in tongues (1 Cor. 14:21). So for that reason, speaking in tongues gives spiritual rest and refreshing to the soul (Matt. 11:28-30). When your soul is weary, being burdened down with fear, anxiety, weakness and the pressures of life, praying in tongues will bring rest, peace and tranquillity and lightness to your soul and it will cause you to be refreshed, invigorated and strengthened, delivering you from the heat of the trials and challenges of life. In times of adversity and trial in my life fraught with anxiety, doubt and discouragement, praying in tongues has calmed my soul and revitalised it with faith, peace and encouragement. There was a personal issue of temptation going on in my life that was causing me frustration in making a decision to follow the pathway that would lead me to doing the will of God. Spending quality time praying in tongues strengthened me to follow God's path. For those groanings, griefs and sorrows that emerge within us as a result of some adversity or challenge in life, the Holy Spirit is there to help us in our weaknesses and to give us the strength to overcome through His intercession.

13

God's Eternal Purpose for the Believer Part 1

"And we know that all things work together for good to them that love God, to them who are the called according to his purpose. For whom he did foreknow, he also did predestinate to be conformed to the image of his Son, that he might be the firstborn among many brethren. Moreover whom he did predestinate, them he also called: and whom he called, them he also justified: and whom he justified, them he also glorified" (Rom. 8:28-30).

I define purpose as an idea, intention, plan, aim, object, design and reason for doing something. The whole creation came into existence for a purpose, and purpose presupposes intelligence, contrary to the evolutionary theory that assumes that every life form and inanimate matter came into being as a result of a big bang. How absurd! According to observation and experience, explosions do not formulate complex life-forms or bring order out of chaos. Similarly, it would be absurd to think that the Oxford Dictionary was the result of an explosion in a bookshop. According to logical reasoning, where there is an organised and ordered complexity of life and matter, they testify to the existence of intelligence and where there is intelligence, there is also purpose.

Human history is filled with purposes, plans, reasons, intentions and designs based on choices. These choices and purposes are reflected in the creative ability and systematic organisation of matter: man-made equipment, buildings, tools, designs etc. In like manner, all of creation reflect the intelligence and creative ability of God, and He has a purpose as to why they were all created. The universe is a reflection of the excellency of God's wisdom and creative ability. The Bible states,

"The heavens declare the glory of God; and the firmament sheweth his handiwork" (Ps. 19:1).

The heavens and the earth are so ordered that men can set and measure time according to the rotation of the earth and the heavenly bodies, to accurately determine days and nights, months, seasons, years; they move within their fixed orbit. This is done by the divine purpose of an intelligent creator (see Gen. 1:14-15). The earth, the moon and the planets have their course of movement around the sun at fixed and precise intervals, to the extent that scientists can predict accurately the next eclipse of the sun. It is on this note that the psalmist declares,

"When I consider the heavens, the work of thy fingers, the moon and the stars, which thou hast ordained" (Ps. 8:3).

The Hebrew rendering of the verb "ordained" is "kun", and it means formed, made, prepared, ready, fixed, certain and right. It signifies to bring something into existence with the consequence of that existence being certain. The term is seldom used to simply mean to bring into existence, but denotes to be firm, fixed or established. The moon and the stars are in their fixed position or fixed station of orbit like the earth and the planets which have their own established routes of orbit around the sun, in accordance with God's preordained plan. Not only has God ordained the existence of the celestial bodies including their course of direction in the heavens, but He has ordained the existence of man and the course of action he must take in life to fulfil his destiny. The same Hebrew word used to speak of the moon and stars being ordained is also employed to refer to the steps of a good man being ordered [Heb. Kun ordained] by the Lord in Psalm 37:23. God has a preordained path for every believer to walk in. If the earth and the planets have their own course of orbiting according to the divine purpose of God, how much so a human being, who is created in the image of God (Gen. 1:26)?

The purpose of God spoken of in Romans 8:28 is alluding to His redemptive plan for the Christian who loves God and who is the called. Every believer who is called is initiated into His redemptive purpose. To fulfil that redemptive purpose, your steps must be ordered by the Lord. The verse actually reads,

"The steps of a good man are ordered by the LORD: and he delighteth in his way" (Ps. 37:23).

The Amplified Bible states in the first clause of this verse: "The steps of a [good] man are directed and established by the Lord..." There is a preordained path that has been prepared for every believer to walk in. Ephesians 2:10 affirms this by declaring,

"For we are God's [own] handiwork (His workmanship), recreated in Christ Jesus, born anew] that we may do those good works which God predestined (planned beforehand) for us [taking paths which he prepared ahead of time], that we should walk in them [living the good life which he prearranged and made ready for us to live" (Amplified Bible).

That is why it is wrong for a Christian believer to try and create his own purpose as if there was no prearranged plan already provided for him to walk in. This is not true Christianity but religious behaviour via self-effort. Purpose was never designed for you to make it happen. But rather, you discover what you were born to accomplish by the revelation of the Spirit. And how do you know that you have found your purpose? You will fit effortlessly into it as a hand fits into a glove made exclusively for it.

How to Discover Your Purpose

To discover your predestined purpose in life, you must make God's Word the highest priority in your life and begin to search out voraciously its hidden treasures of wisdom and knowledge, for in it you will discover your true purpose in life. Become an avid student of the Bible - the Word of God – and do what it teaches. Jesus Christ, our Lord and Saviour, was an example of this very thing so that you would follow in His footsteps. The Messianic passage declares,

"Then said I, Lo, I come (in the volume of the book it is written of me,) to do thy will, O God" (Heb. 10:9).

The writer of Hebrews quotes from Psalm 40: 7 and in verse 8 it also states, "I delight to do thy will, O my God; yea thy law is within my heart." By our Lord's study and meditation of the

Scriptures, He came to understand His purpose which was to become the Saviour of the world through the offering of His body in death (Heb. 10:5-9; Is. 40:6-8). Though Jesus was God Almighty, he laid aside the independent exercise of His Divine attributes of omnipotence, omnipresence and omniscience to become a man who needed to be taught and instructed in the Word of God. Therefore, from childhood to adulthood, the Bible affirms,

"And Jesus increased in wisdom and stature, and in favour with God and man" (Lk. 2:52).

Jesus increased in wisdom through personal study and meditation in the Word and finding passages that spoke about Himself. He also learnt the Old Testament Scriptures by attending His local synagogue every Sabbath as was His custom (Lk. 4:16), and His yearly pilgrimage to the Jewish Temple in Jerusalem (Lk. 2:43-49). Jesus delighted in doing the will of the Father because His Word was in His heart; and so, He was able to do the will of Him who sent Him and to finish His work (Jn. 4:34).

To fulfil God's purpose will require us to come in the volume of the Book which empowers us to do His will and fulfil His purpose. The Book to which I am referring is the Word of God. Coming in the volume of the book involves study, meditation and obedience to its contents. The Bible has been given to us to renew our minds so that we can test, prove and fulfil what is the good, acceptable and perfect will of God (Rom. 12:2).

The Threefold Nature of Divine Purpose

In order to test and approve what the will or purpose of God is, there are three essential things you need to understand and be convinced about concerning His divine purpose for the believer. If any one of these three aspects is missing, it is not God's purpose, but something else. Whatever is being worked out in your life must be consistent with these three following aspects: 1) God's purpose is redemptive; 2) it is for the common good; and 3) it is for the glory of God. Whatever event or circumstance in your life that is incongruous with God's threefold purpose is not of God and should not be embraced.

Firstly, the essence of God's purpose for the believer is redemption from sin, sickness, poverty and the oppression of the Devil (Is. 53:3-5; Matt. 8:16-17; 2 Cor. 8:9; 9:8; Phil. 4:19; 3 Jn. 2). Anything that violates this principle is not of God, but of Satan. Any person who is oppressed by the Devil, all things are not working together for his good but rather for his destruction and harm. Sickness, disease and oppression must be treated in the same way as sin for they both emanate from the same evil root, and were legally removed from us in the redemptive work of Christ (Is. 53:4-5; Matt. 8:16-17 1 Peter 2:24).

Secondly, these kinds of sufferings are not for the common good, they are categorised under the heading of death, evil and cursing according to Deuteronomy 28. But regarding healing, the Bible teaches us,

"How God anointed Jesus of Nazareth with the Holy Ghost and with power: who went about doing good, and healing all that were oppressed of the devil; for God was with him" (Acts 10:38).

Healing is called doing good in the above passage of scripture. Jesus fulfilled God's purpose by ministering for the common good of all for He healed them all. The Bible teaches that the gifts of the Spirit are given for the profit of all. It is written,

"But the manifestation of the Spirit is given to each one for the profit of all" (1 Cor. 12:7 NKJV).

In the Williams New Testament it reads,

"To each of us is given a special spiritual illumination for the common good."

God's purpose in doing good for the benefit of all believers and eventually all mankind is a reflection of His goodness. It is His goodness that leads men to repentance (Rom. 2:4).

Thirdly, God's purpose for the believer brings glory and praise to His Name. The Bible declares,

"Having predestinated us unto the adoption of children by Jesus Christ to himself, according to the good pleasure of his will, To the praise of the glory of his grace..." (Eph. 1:4-5a).

When God's children are delivered from sin, sickness, oppression and fear, that brings glory to the Father and the Name of Jesus (Matt. 9:1-8; Jn. 11:1-4). Furthermore, there are adversities that God has ordained to work together for our good and fulfil the purpose of God. Since they fulfil the purpose of God, they will not contradict the provisions of the redemptive work of Christ. Adversities that work together for good will be consistent with the threefold purpose of God so what is thought or planned for evil, God has purposed it for good (Gen. 50:20). And the adversities I am referring to are temptations, trials, persecution and martyrdom for righteousness and the Name of Jesus. Suffering for the sake of the Gospel entails the threefold purpose of God: it is redemptive; it is for the common good, and it glorifies God.

Christ's sufferings were redemptive and for the common good so that men would be saved (Jn. 3:14-17). Jesus said,

"...I am come that they might have life, and that they might have it more abundantly. I am the good shepherd: the good shepherd giveth his life for the sheep" (Jn. 10:10a-11).

The context show us that Jesus' purpose for coming was so that we may have life in abundance, and the next verse affirms how this would be done: by giving His life for the sheep. In learning obedience experientially through the things He suffered, He became the Author of eternal salvation to those who obeyed Him (Heb. 5:8-9). Hence, in His sufferings, He brought glory to God. Therefore, He said,

"...The hour is come, that the Son of man should be glorified. Verily, verily, I say unto you, Except a corn of wheat fall into the ground and die, it abideth alone: but if it die, it bringeth forth much fruit...Now is my soul troubled; and what shall I say? Father save me from this hour: but for this cause came I unto this hour. Father glorify thy name..." (Jn. 12:23b-24, 27-28a).

The hour spoken of here is the hour of Christ's sufferings and death, because in the following verse, Jesus compares His hour of suffering to a grain of wheat falling into the ground and dying. But His death will fulfil the redemptive purpose of God and bring forth much fruit unto salvation, and in this the Father and the Son are glorified (Heb. 2:9-10). Similarly, the sufferings of the saints in temptation, persecution, trials and martyrdom for the sake of Christ glorifies God because it has some redemptive benefit. The Bible declares,

"having your conversation [manner of life] honest among the Gentiles: that, whereas they speak against you as evil doers, they may by your good works, which they shall behold, glorify God in the day of visitation" (1 Peter 2:12).

Other biblical references show us that suffering for the Name of Jesus glorifies God (Jn. 21:18-19; 1 Peter 4:12-14, 16). By the saints doing good in the midst of sufferings, many of the enemies of the Gospel become converted as they behold your good works as intimated in the above passage of scripture. Furthermore, temptations, trials and persecution serve to strengthen and perfect godly character through holy resistance called endurance (Ja. 1:2-4). This is included in all things working together for the good of the believer. But there is a condition on this comprehensive promise that is twofold: firstly, you must love God and secondly, you must be the called according to His redemptive purpose; and only then, can all things work together in your favour. The "called" spoken of in this verse is referring to the effectual call that identifies who is chosen in contrast to the general call not responded to (Matt. 20:16; Rom. 8:29-30).

The next chapter will clarify the purpose for which we are called as briefly stated in Romans 8:29. It is the destiny of every believer who has responded to His call.

14

God's Eternal Purpose for the Believer Part 2

Following the previous chapter, God has an eternal purpose for the believer to fulfil, and verse 29 sums up what that divine purpose is, and it states,

"For whom he did foreknow, he also did predestinate to be conformed to the image of his Son, that he might be the firstborn among many brethren."

God's purpose is twofold: to conform us to the image of His Son, Jesus Christ, and that He might be the Firstborn among many brethren. This purpose encapsulates the Divine and human aspects. Our primary destiny in Christ is to be fashioned according to the image of God's Son; to be as He is and to walk as He walked and to demonstrate that he has the pre-eminence among His brethren as the Firstborn.

There are three successive stages of conformity to the image of Christ. The first stage can be seen in our initial conversion by faith in Christ and His redemptive work on the cross. When we repented of our sins and received Christ as our Lord and Saviour, our nature was changed from old to new. The Bible puts it like this:

"That ye put off concerning the former conversation [the manner of life] the old man, which is corrupt according to the deceitful lusts; and be renewed in the spirit of your mind; and that ye put on the new man, which after God is created in righteousness and true holiness... Lie not one to another, seeing that ye have put off the old man with his deeds; And have put on the new man, which is renewed in knowledge after the image of him that created him" (Eph. 4:22-24; col. 3:9-10).

When we received Christ in our hearts, we did put off the old man with its sinful life and deeds and did put on the new man, created in righteousness and true holiness, which are according to the image of Him who created him. This change took place when we were renewed by knowledge in the spirit of our minds. And so now, we are a new creation in Christ Jesus, old things have passed away and all things have become new (2 Cor. 5:17).

We now carry the image of Christ in our renewed spirit, and that image is righteousness and true holiness. The Bible declares that we are the righteousness of God in Christ Jesus (2 Cor. 5:21) and called saints of which the Greek rendering is "hagioi", meaning "holy ones," sanctified and purified by the blood of Jesus Christ. In putting on the new man, we also put on the Lord Jesus Christ. We have become partakers of His divine nature (2 Peter 1:4), therefore the Bible states,

"herein is our love made perfect, that we may have boldness in the day of judgment: because AS HE IS, SO ARE WE IN THIS WORLD" (1 Jn. 4:17).

Understanding who you are in Christ will catapult you into the second stage of your development in Christ; and this has to do with coming into spiritual maturity so that the perfect image you have in Christ will have full expression in your thoughts, your words and your deeds. Bearing the image of Christ in your spirit needs to be transitioned into the realm of your soul, and this is accomplished by the renewing of your mind as intimated in Romans 12:2,

"And be not conformed to this world: but be ye transformed by the renewing of your mind, that ye may prove what is that good, and acceptable, and perfect will of God."

Once the nature has been changed through the new birth, you then need to change your old thought patterns that were left behind by the old nature when you became born-again. The new birth instantly deals with the old man (the old nature), but the study and meditation of the Word of God progressively deals with the old thought-patterns. The Greek verb for "transformed" is "metamorphousthe", which denotes the imperfect and present tense. This signifies a past continuous action and a present continuous action, indicating that we are in the process of being transformed

The progressive transformation of the believer in the image of Christ is being done through the Word. As we behold the perfect image of the Lord in us by the mirror of the Word, we are being changed from glory to glory by the Spirit of the Lord (2 Cor. 3:18).

God's Eternal Purpose for the Believer Part 2

The purpose of the fivefold ministry of apostles, prophets, evangelists, pastors and teachers is to bring the whole Church into the measure of the stature of the fullness of Christ (Eph. 4:11-13). It is the destiny and purpose to which every believer has been predestined to accomplish.

The third stage of our conformity to the image of Christ is corporeal. When the Lord Jesus Christ shall appear in glory, we shall be changed to partake of the corporeal image of the heavenly. The Bible declares it in this manner,

"For our conversation is in heaven; from whence also we look for the Saviour, the Lord Jesus Christ: Who shall change our vile body, that it may be fashioned like unto his glorious body,..." (Phil. 3:20-21a).

By our bodies being changed from mortal to immortality, we shall become like Him as 1 John 3:2 states,

"Beloved, now are we the sons of God, and it doth not appear what we shall be: but we know that, when he shall appear, we shall be like him; for we shall see him as he is."

This is the glorification of the saints; as Christ was glorified (Jn. 7:39; Phil. 3:21), the saints will also be glorified with Him. When the last trumpet shall sound, the mystery of God announces that we shall be changed in a moment in the twinkling of an eye, and we shall put on incorruption, and so the fullness of our conformity to the image of Christ will be accomplished (1 Cor. 15:51-54). Being transitioned from glory to glory will climax at the resurrection and transfiguration of the saints, the destiny of our glorification; hence the following verse lists the saints being glorified as the last thing in a series of events,

"Moreover whom he did predestinate, them he also called: and whom he called, them he also justified: and whom he justified, them he also glorified".

But before expounding more on this, I want to conclude in explaining the last clause of verse 29 which states,

"...that he might be the firstborn among many brethren."

This verse refers to Jesus Christ being the firstborn among many brethren. The term "brethren" here describes His disciples who believe in Him throughout the ages (see Jn. 21:17; Matt. 25:31-33, 35-40). Christ being the firstborn among many brethren alludes to the fact that he is a brother among many brethren. He is spiritually our brother and we are His brethren. Hebrews 2:11-12 affirms,

"For both he that sanctifieth and they who are sanctified are all of one: for which cause he [Christ] is not ashamed to call them brethren, Saying, I will declare thy name unto my brethren, in the midst of the church will I sing praise unto thee."

Furthermore, the firstborn was always identified from among the brothers of a family. Since Jesus Christ is our brother and we are His brethren, he has been predestinated to be the firstborn among many brethren. To apprehend Him as the firstborn, you need to understand the laws and customs of the firstborn rights and inheritance from the Old Testament for the Law is a shadow of spiritual realities (Heb. 10:1; Col. 2:16-17).

The term "firstborn" is used in Scripture firstly, to speak of the physical birth of the first male child in a family, and secondly, as reference to the legal status, position and the birthright inheritance. There were two specific rights and privileges that the firstborn received as his birthright: 1) he had bequeathed to him a double portion of his father's inheritance; and 2) he succeeded his father as head over the family (Deut. 21:15-17). An exalted position of authority and dignity was bestowed upon the firstborn who preceded all his male siblings. And so by analogy, Jesus Christ is the firstborn among His redeemed brethren because he is before all things which gives Him the right to have the pre-eminence and the headship over the redeemed, the Church and all creation.

In the book of Colossians, it states,

"Who is the image of the invisible God, the firstborn of every creature [Gk all creation]: For by him were all things created, that are in heaven, and that are in earth, visible and invisible, whether they be thrones, or dominions, or principalities, or powers: all things were created by him and for him: And he is before all things, and by him all things consist. And he is the head of the body, the church: who is the beginning, the firstborn from the dead; that in all things, he might have the pre-eminence" (Col. 1:15-18).

God has predestined His true believers to be conformed to the image of His Son, Jesus Christ; to what end? That He may be manifested to and through His Church as the glorified and exalted Lord possessing all authority and power over all creation to the praise of the glory of God. This is God's ultimate purpose for the believer. His counsel will stand and His eternal purpose will certainly come to pass; no man, devil or circumstance will frustrate His divine purpose. He will fulfil His eternal purpose through His Church for they have been predestined to do so. Verse 29a-30 states,

"For whom he did foreknow, he also did predestinate...whom he did predestinate, them he also called: and whom he called, them he also justified: and whom he justified: them he also glorified."

To comprehend and appreciate what the scriptural passage is saying, you must understand the biblical concept of foreknowledge and predestination. Both are comprehensive concepts that include all things: visible and invisible, all forms of life, inanimate matter, events, circumstances, divine and human intervention etc. They are both all-inclusive notions.

Foreknowledge is an aspect of God's omniscience and it is defined to be His perfect knowledge from eternity of the certainty of all things that will come to pass. The Bible affirms,

"known unto God are ALL his works from the beginning of creation" (Acts 15:19).

His foreknowledge is not perfect knowledge of possibilities, but actualities that are inevitable. For example, God's foreknowledge – knowledge beforehand – of the crucifixion of Christ as declared in 1 Peter 1:19,

"But with the precious blood of Christ, as of a lamb without blemish and without spot: who was verily foreordained before the foundation of the world, but was manifest in these last times for you."

The term "foreordained" has been generally mistranslated from the Greek word "proginosko" which means "foreknown". It has, however, been correctly translated in the Revised Version of the Bible. Although the error is not grave, there is a minor difference, even though both terms are closely related. God's foreknowledge of the inevitable and certain outcome of all things is due to the fact that they have been foreordained or predestined to come to pass. Whatever God foreknows is because He has ordained it to come to pass. In Biblical Theology, this subject comes under the heading entitled "The decrees of God in General" (A. A. Hodge 1860).

Predestinate is from the Greek rendering "proorizo", meaning to mark out or determine before, thus indicating to select, determine, ordain or to appoint beforehand. While predestination is comprehensive, election is one aspect of it. Election refers to the choosing of a people to be redeemed by the blood of Christ to make up His chosen and peculiar people, ruled over by His Son Jesus Christ, for all eternity. The Scriptures sets forth predestination and election as it relates to redemption:

"According as he hath chosen us in him [Christ] before the foundation of the world, that we should be holy and without blame before him in love: Having predestinated us unto the adoption of children by Jesus Christ to himself, according to the good pleasure of his will...In whom also we have obtained an inheritance, being predestinated according to the purpose of him who worketh all things after the counsel of his own will" (Eph. 1:4-5, 11).

When the Apostle Paul spoke of predestination in Romans 8:29-30, he was referring to it from the aspect of redemptive election whereby He chose us before the foundation of the world unto salvation by Jesus Christ according to His sovereign grace and purpose. It is erroneous to think that God looked down through time and saw that we would believe and therefore chose us. That would not be God choosing you but rather you consenting to your choice of Him and therefore salvation would be by works and not by grace. To be biblically correct, election is the cause of salvation; men's response to believe is the effect. Predestination is the basis upon which we believe to be saved. The Word of God purports,

"And when the Gentiles heard this, they were glad, and glorified the word of the Lord: and as many as were ordained to eternal life believed" (Acts 13:48).

When the subject of predestination and election are put in the correct biblical context, it does not seem harsh. Moreover that context is this: in God's eternal and redemptive plan, he not only predestinates the events or consequences, but also the means by which they are accomplished, such as the preachers of truth, the ministry of the Holy Spirit, the prayers of the saints and the free choices of men to respond to the Gospel. There are two sides to predestination: the divine responsibility and the human responsibility. In the divine responsibility, God elects and calls and saves the sinner; in the human responsibility, the sinner makes the choice to respond to God's call. These two sides are intimated in 2 Thessalonians 2:13,

"but we are bound to give thanks always to God for you, brethren beloved of the Lord, because God hath from the beginning chosen you to salvation through sanctification of the Spirit and belief of the truth."

This verse clearly shows us that biblical predestination or election includes man's free choice, otherwise it is fatalism – the preclusion of free choice to determine one's destiny. The above verse declares that from the beginning, God has chosen us to salvation, and it was manifested through the work of the Spirit who sanctified us, cleansing us from sin (Eph. 5:26; 1 Cor. 6:11; Tit. 3:5). Without the convicting work and sanctifying power of the Spirit, men would be unable to respond to the Gospel and live uprightly because their freewill would be enslaved to the dictates of their depraved nature (Rom. 3:9-12). Jesus, in His discourse with the Jews, said,

"No man can come to me except the Father which hath sent me draw him: and I will raise him up at the last day. It is written in the prophets, And they shall be all taught of God. Every man that hath heard, and hath learned of the Father, cometh unto me" (Jn. 6:44-45).

Unregenerate men are incapable of coming to Christ by themselves, it requires the inward work of the Spirit of the Father. Therefore it is important to understand that we do not choose Him, it is He that chose us (Jn. 15:16). The Bible firmly states,

"Who hath saved us, and called us with an holy calling, not according to our works, but according to his own purpose and grace, which was given us in Christ Jesus before the world began" (2 Tim. 1:9).

We were elected because of His sovereign grace, not because of our works or who we were. Grace makes void our own works for if it is grace, it is no more of works (see Rom. 9:10-13; 11:5-6).

The last clause of 2 Thessalonians 2:13 sets forth the human responsibility: "...the belief of the truth." Under the influence of God's grace, men must respond in order to be saved by believing the truth that is preached, for salvation is by grace through faith (Eph. 2:8). God's eternal plan will never exclude the responsibility to believe. And when a person believes the truth, he will see that God had elected him before the foundation of the world. On Judgment Day, no one will be able to make the excuse that they did not make it into God's Kingdom because they were not elected. Whosoever puts their faith in Jesus Christ, it will mean that they were elected to salvation before the world began. The apostle concludes the concept of predestination inferring that when God did predestinate from eternity, we were also called, justified and glorified, for He declares the end from the beginning (Is. 46:10).

Finally, our election is based on the merits of Christ's righteousness, obedience and sacrificial death on the Cross, thus creating us unto good works (Eph. 2:10).

15

The All-Sufficiency of Christ

"What shall we then say to these things? If God be for us, who can be against us? He that spared not his own Son, but delivered him up for us all, how shall he not with him freely give us all things?" (Rom. 8:31-32)

The Apostle Paul presents a question pertaining to all that he wrote about in the preceding verses concerning God's eternal purpose, foreknowledge, predestination, calling, justification and glorification (v28-30). The answer he gives regarding these things alludes to the fact that if God is for us, who can be against us? It is to this that the apostle expounds upon in the subsequent verses (v32-39). He asserts that there is none who can charge guilt to God's elect since it is He who has justified them (v30, 33). Neither can any condemn them because Christ died for them and rose again and is now at the right hand of God making intercession for us (v34). The chapter concludes by stating emphatically that no one or anything can separate us from the love of God in Christ Jesus (v35-39). By these statements, the writer explains, "If God be for us, who can be against us?"

The underlying theme that transpires through my mind when I read the opening passage of this scripture is "The All-Sufficiency of Christ", whereby nothing is missing, or uncovered; neither is lacking in the Person of Jesus Christ and His redemptive work on the Cross. Everything has been paid for. His resounding words continue to echo through the ages: "It is finished" (Jn. 19:30). This phrase is translated from the Greek verb "tetelestai" and its verbal form is in the perfect tense, which indicates a past action or state which has a continuous or ongoing result. The Greek meaning is, to bring to an end; to complete or fulfil; to accomplish something. When Jesus spoke from the cross, "It is finished", and then died (Jn. 19:30), there were several things that He brought to an end: 1) He brought to an end the Law of commandments that were against us, nailing it to His Cross (Col. 2:14); 2) He brought an end to the passing over of sins through the forbearance of God in the Old Testament sacrificial system (Rom. 3:25-26); 3) Christ brought an end to types and shadows by fulfilling them (Matt. 5:17; Col. 2:16-17; Heb. 10:1-3); and 4) He brought an end to the Law's demand for righteousness by fulfilling it (Rom. 10:3).

According to the perfect tense of the Greek verb – a past state or action with a continuous result – Jesus Christ died once for all, and his death has produced a continuing result of redemption for all who believe. The Bible declares,

"Neither by the blood of goats and calves, but by his own blood he entered in once into the holy place, having obtained eternal redemption for us...By the which will we are sanctified through the offering of the body of Jesus Christ once for all" (Heb. 9:12; 10:10).

Jesus Christ offered up Himself in death once for all and entered once into the holy place of heaven, unlike the blood of bulls and goats offered yearly by the high priest which could not take away sin, therefore there was not an end of sacrifices being offered for sins. Every year there was a remembrance of sins. And for this reason no high priest could ever say in the perfect tense, "It is finished", until the perfect sacrifice and the perfect High Priest arrived, who would make an end of transgressions and bring in everlasting righteousness by the remission of sins (Dan. 9:24).

Next, it is important to answer the question as to why the sacrifice of Jesus Christ was so perfect, complete and all-sufficient for every human being throughout history past, present and future. The answer lies in the opening verse of this chapter and it reads,

"He that spared not his own Son, but delivered him up for us all, how shall he not with him also freely give us all things?" (Rom. 8:32)

The Gift that God gave for the salvation of men was invaluable and priceless. He did not give an animal sacrifice, or a mere man, or an angel, neither the most expensive inanimate material thing in the world. He gave His most precious Gift when He gave His own Son – this was His best. Just to reiterate, He gave His own Son who was of infinite value in the sight of God.

Jesus Christ is the Son of God, but to understand the true value of His Person, you need to be cognizant of His full title as expressed in the Johannine literature which is "the only begotten Son of God, His only begotten Son or the only begotten of the Father" (e.g. Jn. 3:16, 18; 1:14, 18). The Greek term for "only begotten" is "monogenes", literally meaning "one kind", because He is the Son of God who is the only One of His kind. There is no one in God's Kingdom or in all creation who bears the title "only begotten Son of God". Its meaning is exclusive to Jesus Christ and surpasses all holy and redeemed men and holy angelic hosts who are called sons of God (Gen. 6:2, 4; Job 1:6; 2:1;38:7; Matt. 5:9; Rom. 8:14, 16; Gal. 4:5-7). It is also interesting to note when sonship is applied to men or angels, it is virtually used in the plural noun to convey that God has many sons, but when used of Jesus Christ, it is invariably used in the singular form, intimating the uniqueness and superiority of Christ's Sonship and relationship with God the Father. The nature of that Sonship and relationship is coequal with God the Father.

The term "Son" related to "God" by use of the genitive, thus, becoming the phrase "Son of God". In Hebrew idiomatic expression, this signifies to be in the nature and essence of. To give a few examples, prophets in the Old Testament were called "sons of the prophets"; the term was not alluding to their pedigree or natural descent, but referred to the nature and destiny of their calling to be prophets (2 Kgs. 2:3; 4:38; 9:1, 4). Note that other genitive expressions are used to depict the nature, character or destiny of a person such as sons of disobedience, sons of wrath (Eph. 2:2-3; son of peace (Lk. 10:6); son of hell (Matt. 23:15) and sons of men (Ps. 115:16). And so when the term "only begotten Son of God" is applied to Christ, it denotes His divine equality, His Deity and eternal essence as God (Jn. 1:1-3, 14, 18; Rom. 9:5; Heb. 1:9). Furthermore, Jesus' claim to be the Son of God was understood by His contemporaries – the Jews and their religious leaders – as claiming equality with God, and therefore was wrongly accused of blasphemy (Jn. 5:18; 10:30-37; Matt. 26:63-65; Mk. 14:61-64).

The All-Sufficiency of Christ

Unlike Christ the Son of the living God, the redeemed are the sons of God, begotten (Ja. 1:18; 1 Jn. 5:1-3); born again (Jn. 1:12-13; 3:3-8; 1 Peter 1:23); and adopted (Rom. 8:14-15; Gal. 4:4-7). As sons of God, we partake of His divine nature in a moral, ethical and spiritual sense (2 Peter 1:4; 1 Jn. 4:7); we are never made Deity like the Son of God who was never begotten, created or adopted. God the Father's statement in prophecy, "...Thou art my Son; this day have I begotten thee" (Ps. 2:7), has reference to His bodily resurrection and not His birth as some wrongly purport (Acts 13:32-33). He is the eternal Son of God. So when God spared not His own Son but delivered Him up as a sacrifice for us, he gave us a gift that was of infinite and eternal value that would eradicate the sins of all time: past, present and future would never lose its efficacy and power to redeem. An eternal value brings about an eternal inheritance that will never cease (Heb. 9:15).

Because Christ is the Eternal Son of God coequal with God, He is All-Sufficient in His Person and His sacrificial work on the Cross. There is no need or problem that His death did not cover. Every solution lies in the All-Sufficiency of Christ. He has provided all things in His redemptive work. And the fact that God gave us His Son - His most treasured possession - how much less His spiritual and temporal blessings which are nothing to be compared in value to His own Son. He has already proven that he is willing to give us all things because He gave us something far greater: Son. The Bible reads,

"Blessed be the God and Father of our Lord Jesus Christ, who hath blessed us with all spiritual blessings in heavenly places in Christ" (Eph. 1:3).

When you already have Christ, you have everything, for everything is in Him (2 Cor. 1:20). Whether it is righteousness, peace, deliverance, joy healing and health, financial prosperity, heaven, protection, immortality, authority, power etc., it is all in Him. And God desires you to experience His provision of all things for they are already yours. The Word of God confirms,

"Therefore let no man glory in men. For all things are yours; Whether Paul, or Apollos, or Cephas, or the world, or life, or death, or things present, or things to come; all are yours; And ye are Christ's and Christ is God's" (1 Cor. 3:21-23).

The Father freely giving us all things is rooted and motivated in His amazing and unsurpassing love for us as declared in St John 3:16,

"For God so loved the world, that he gave his only begotten Son, that whosoever believeth in him should not perish, but have everlasting life."

The greatness of His provision is determined by the greatness of His love, and apprehending that love will catapult you into the greatness of His provision. He has given us His Spirit to help us know by revelation, things that God has prepared for those who love Him (1 Cor. 2:9-12). The extent of your love for God will be determined by the degree to which you understand His love for you; and that love is revealed in His Son (1 Jn. 4:9-10, 19).

Since the Son of God is God Almighty, that makes His sacrificial offering to be of infinite value, able to encompass all people for all time. The blood of Christ is referred to in Acts 20:28 as God's blood, and that blood represents the life of the sinless Son of

God which is of infinite value in the sight of God. That infinite quality of life has been given to every believer in Christ; it is everlasting life – a life that is exceedingly abundant in enduring quality. He has given us His Life. The Bible reads,

"The thief cometh not but for to steal, and to kill, and to destroy. I am come that they might have life, and that they might have it more abundantly" (Jn. 10:10).

Jesus' Godhood constitutes the value of His Person and His redemptive work to be exclusive (Jn. 14:6; Acts 4:12), all-sufficient and encompassing (Eph. 1:3; Col. 2:10). We have received of His fullness, and the fullness He possesses is grace and truth according as the scriptural passage reads,

"...the glory as of the only begotten of the Father,) full of grace and truth...And of his fullness have all received, and grace for grace. For the law was given by Moses, but grace and truth came by Jesus Christ" (Jn. 1:14b, 16-17).

Jesus Christ possesses an infinite, endless supply of grace for every person and every need that will never run out. It is able to fill us up and overflow because it stems from an unlimited Source of supply. His grace is exceedingly wealthy. He has quickened us to life,

"That in the ages to come he might shew the exceeding riches of his grace in his kindness towards us through Jesus Christ" (Eph. 2:7).

We have on the inside of us an endless resource of blessings that far exceeds our understanding and expectation that is yet to be tapped into. There are two basic aspects to the grace of God. Firstly, it is the unmerited favour of God demonstrated in His approval, goodwill, mercy and love towards undeserving sinners who receive Him, by faith, based on the merits of Christ's Person and redemptive work (Eph. 2:8-9). Secondly, the grace of God is the enabling power and strength of God to do the impossible and supernatural. Grace is the divine ability to be and to do what truth requires of you; hence the Apostle Paul writes the Lord's words spoken to him in his time of severe persecution and adversity,

"And he said unto me, My grace is sufficient for thee: for my strength is made perfect in weakness. Most gladly therefore will I rather glory in my infirmities that the power of Christ may rest upon me" (2 Cor. 12:9).

In this passage, the apostle equates the grace of Christ with the power of Christ (see also 2 Tim. 2:1). It has the ability to eradicate any problem or challenge in life because it is all-sufficient and has many facets that constitutes it as being all-sufficient, hence the reason why it is called in Scripture "the manifold grace of God" (1 Peter 4:10), and that grace gives us an abundance of everything. Its multi-faceted nature supplies righteousness, peace, joy, divine ability, giftings, wisdom and knowledge, health, protection, victory over temptations, financial prosperity, favourable opportunities that no man can stop, promotion etc. Jesus Christ has given us every facet of His grace through His redemption on the Cross. The Scripture reads,

"For ye know the grace of our Lord Jesus Christ, that, though he was rich, yet for your sakes, he became poor, that ye through his poverty might be rich...And God is able to make all grace abound toward you; that ye, always having all sufficiency in all things, may abound unto every good work" (2 Cor. 8:9; 9:8).

To enjoy the all-sufficiency of God's grace is going to require faith on your part; for faith is the channel or conduit through which the grace of God flows from Him to us (Rom. 5:2; Eph. 2:8). We grow in the efficacy of God's grace through faith in our lives by acknowledging every good thing that resides in us in Christ Jesus (Philm. 1:6).

Grace in the above passage of scripture is a metonymy for giving, whether spiritually, physically or financially. Jesus Christ who was rich and wealthy, temporarily gave up the privileges and prerogatives of the infinite glory of heaven and made a descent to earth in the form of a man and became obedient unto death, giving His sinless life for our sake so that we may be exalted from spiritual, physical and financial poverty to the opposite corresponding wealth (3 Jn. 2). The context of the passage is about finances, the principle of wealth can also apply to every facet of human life. Biblical prosperity is holistic. A person who is rich financially is not truly rich according to biblical definition. There are people who are rich, but yet, they are unhappy, unfulfilled and dissatisfied with their lives; the reason is: they have not received Christ as their all-sufficiency. True biblical prosperity and wealth begins with a divine relationship with Jesus Christ from which every spiritual and temporal blessing emanates. And the nature of God's blessings will bring self-sufficiency into your life and surpassing to bless others. In 2 Corinthians 9:8 of the Amplified Bible reads,

"And God is able to make all grace (every favour and earthly blessing) come to you in abundance, so that you may always and under all circumstances and whatever the need be self-sufficient [possessing enough to require no aid or support and furnished in abundance for every good work and charitable donation]".

16

How to be Victorious Over the Condemnation of the Devil

"Who shall lay anything to the charge of God's elect? It is God that justifieth. Who is he that condemneth? It is Christ that died, yea rather, that is risen again, who is even at the right hand of God, who also maketh intercession for us" (Rom. 8:33-34).

In our Christian walk of faith, we are engaged in spiritual warfare against an archenemy who is seeking to destroy our souls. The Bible describes him as a roaring lion who walks about seeking whom he may devour (1 Peter 5:8). However, if he is unable to destroy your soul, he will try to destroy your effectiveness as a disciple of Jesus Christ. One particular strategy he uses to ensure you do not enjoy the blessings of your salvation and the power of their influence on the world purchased by the blood of Jesus Christ, is to bring you under condemnation through his lies, deceit and trickery.

In order not to succumb to his power of suggestion, you must know the enemy and his devices lest he has the advantage over you (2 Cor. 2:11). Ignorance is the Devil's playing field where he has the power over many believers. Ignorance is where the enemy thrives that is why he and his cohorts are called in Scripture "world-rulers of the darkness of this age" (Eph. 6:12 Greek). They are world-rulers because the world has been covered with their darkness. Darkness is a metaphor for ignorance. The whole world of humanity is lost in sin and destruction because they do not know the truth according as it is written,

"But if our gospel be hid, it is hid to them that are lost: In whom the god of this world hath blinded the minds of them which believe not...This I say therefore, and testify in the Lord, that ye henceforth walk not as other Gentiles walk, in the vanity of their mind, Having the understanding darkened, being alienated from the life of God through the ignorance that is in them, because of the blindness of their heart" (2 Cor. 4:3-4a; Eph. 4:17-18).

According to the above, the reason why Satan is the god of this world is because he has blinded the minds of those who believe not. His key strategy is to attack and influence the mind and heart through deception; hence, they are made vain in their minds; their understand is darkened; they are ignorant and blind in their hearts, and are therefore alienated from the life of God as stated in the above. Divine life is absent from men's human existence because of the darkness – the ignorance that pervades their minds and hearts.

Nevertheless, the antidote to delivering people from spiritual darkness is the light of God's Word. It is the light that will expel the darkness, for light is more powerful than darkness. That is true in the spiritual as well as in the natural. Darkness prevails simply because the light is absent. However, when light is present, the darkness has to flee. The Bible reads,

"And the light shineth in darkness; and the darkness comprehended it not" (Jn. 1:5).

The Greek rendering for "comprehend" is "katalambano", and it means to lay hold of, to apprehend or seize upon with the sense of overpowering. Metaphorically, the darkness has never overpowered the light, neither does it have the ability to understand, perceive or apprehend with the mind, the mysteries of the light.

To remove the darkness or ignorance from the mind is going to require you to expose your mind to the light of God's Word, because the entrance of His words give light by giving understanding unto the simple (Ps. 119:130). The sinner who is already under condemnation needs to a) receive spiritual illumination about his own condition; b) acknowledge that Jesus has taken the punishment for his sins; c) believe in the Name of the Son of God which will translate him from condemnation to life (Jn. 3:17-18). Those who are born again and positioned in Christ need to know who they are in Christ and what Christ accomplished for them in the finished work of redemption (Rom. 8:1-3).

The condemnation that Christians feel about something they just did or had done many years ago still come to haunt them, even after being forgiven by God. These symptoms are not proof that they are under condemnation or divine judgment, given the fact that the Scriptures tell that there is no more condemnation to those who are in Christ Jesus (Rom. 8:1). Rather, the symptoms are evidence that they have surrendered to the lies and deceptions of the Devil which are designed to keep the believer from enjoying his benefits in Christ. In order to counteract these lies of the Devil, who is called "the accuser of the brethren" (Rev. 12:10), there are four main truths, given in Romans 8:33-34), which are essential to know, concerning your redemption. This knowledge will expel the darkness from your minds:

- the God who only has the authority to acquit or condemn to eternal damnation is for us

- the basis upon which that acquittal has taken place is the sacrificial death of Christ

- the resurrection of Christ confirms that Christ's sacrificial death was accepted

- Christ is seated at the right hand of the throne of God continually making intercession for us.

Renewing your mind to these four main truths will liberate the Christian to be all that God has called him to be. I want to expound on each truth in detail.

The God who has the authority to acquit or condemn to eternal damnation is for us. God is the righteous Judge of heaven and earth; His judgments are always based on truth and justice. He can never be wrong, unjust or untruthful. Whatever he decrees or establishes is legally, ethically and morally right. One of the aspects of God's nature is that He cannot lie (Num. 23:19; Heb. 6:18). The Bible affirms,

"He is the Rock, his work is perfect: for all his ways are judgment: a God of truth and without iniquity, just and right is he" (Deut. 32:4).

The Amplified Bible expounds and expands on the meaning in the original Hebrew text by stating,

"He is the Rock, His work is perfect, for all His ways are law and justice. A God of faithfulness without breach or deviation, just and right is He."

Concerning the Divine nature and character of God, the verse intimates God as being perfect in His works and all His ways are law and justice. God does not make decisions based on some whim or arbitrary volition, but according to this scripture, He decrees with consistent regard to His law and justice revealed in the Word of God. As creation operates consistently according to God's established laws, the realm of the Spirit functions likewise (Jer. 31:35-36). God has promised and decreed in His Word regarding His people,

"Behold the days come, saith the LORD, that I will make a new covenant with the house of Israel, and with the house of Judah...But this shall be the covenant that I will make with the house of Israel...for I will forgive their iniquity, and I will remember their sins no more" (Jer. 31:31, 33a, 34c).

A covenant is a binding agreement that cannot be annulled by anything that comes afterwards (read Gal. 3:15). It cannot be altered or changed. Now with respect to God, His Covenant cannot be annulled, altered or changed. God says in His Word,

"My covenant will I not break, nor alter the thing that is gone out of my lips" (Ps. 89:34).

With regard to the New Covenant, the thing that has gone out of His lips is, "I will forgive their iniquity, and I will remember their sins no more" (v34c). This promise is initiated in His love and mercy, and once spoken becomes law and justice. This covenant-promise was ratified in the blood of Jesus (Matt. 26:28). God cannot break His Covenant because He is faithful, without breach or deviation (Deut. 32:4 Amp.). So when God declares in His Word,

"If we confess our sins, he is faithful and just to forgive us our sins, and to cleanse us from all unrighteousness" (1 Jn. 1:9),

this verse is truth and is part of the New Covenant - believe it and do it. Do not allow your feelings to dictate what is truth; let the Word of God be your rule of faith for living. Be dictated to by the Word of God for it is the truth. Receive your assurance of forgiveness from the promises in God's Word and refuse to accept any feelings of condemnation for they are merely symptoms designed by the Devil to deceive you. Resist those symptoms by faith and they will flee from you (Ja. 4:7).

Note, the Devil does what is in his nature, for his name "Devil" is from the Greek word "diabolos", which means a malicious slanderer; an accuser; and furthermore, Jesus calls him "a liar and the father of it" (Jn. 8:44) because he did not remain in the truth. Whatever accusation the Devil hurls at you that contradicts the Word of God is a lie designed to deceive you. If you are presented with the Gospel by which you can be saved or you are already born again by the Word of truth (Ja. 1:17; 1 Peter 1:23), dismiss the doubts and believe the Word of God. Jesus says to continue in His Word and you shall know the truth and the truth shall make you free (Jn. 8:31-32).

The truth says that you are the righteousness of God in Christ (2 Cor. 5:21), and that there is no more condemnation to those who are in Christ Jesus (Rom. 8:1), and that if God be for you, who can be against you (Rom. 8:31). If the one who is for you is the justifier or acquitter of our sins, then the basis upon which he does so is the substitutionary death of Christ.

Just to reiterate the Apostle Paul's statement in verse 34: "Who is he that condemneth? It is Christ that died." God's declaration of righteousness over us is due to the fact that Christ was put to death for us, and so the blood of Jesus Christ has washed away our sins and declared us righteous before God. A divine and legal exchange transpired at the cross. Jesus took our guilt and liability for punishment so that we may obtain His righteousness. Since sin has been condemned and punished in the sinless Son of God (1 Peter 2:24), that shows God to be just to forgive us of our sins and cleanse us in the Blood of Christ. If Christ had not come to die, He would be unjust to forgive us because there would be no legal basis to do so. But Christ came to die and shed His blood to satisfy God's righteous demand for justice against sin so that he might be just and the justifier of all who believe in Jesus (Rom. 3:25-26). And that is why the Bible declares,

"but if we walk in the light, as he is in the light, we have fellowship one with another, and the blood of Jesus Christ his Son cleanseth us from all sin...If we confess our sins, he is faithful and JUST to forgive us our sins, and to cleanse us from all unrighteousness" (1 Jn. 1:7, 9).

Since God is faithful to do what He promised (Heb. 10:23), and just to perform what He legally made provision for, God's forgiveness and cleansing are certain. Convince your heart of this true reality by meditating in the Word instead of the lies of the enemy. The Christian brethren, whom the Devil accused before God day and night, overcame those accusations by the blood of the Lamb and by the word of their testimony (Rev. 12:10-11). When the Devil is throwing accusations at you, overcome them by testifying in faith to yourself and the Devil about what the blood has purchased for you, and he will flee from you (Ja. 4:7).

While we are justified by His blood (Rom. 5:9), we are also justified by His resurrection (Rom. 4:25). The following clause reads, "...yea rather, that is risen again..." (Rom. 8:34). His resurrection testifies to the fact that his sacrificial death on the Cross rendered inactive the power of death according to Hebrews 2:14,

"forasmuch then as the children are partakers of flesh and blood, he also himself likewise took part of the same, that through death he might destroy him that had the power of death, that is, the devil."

The word "destroy" in this passage is from the Greek rendering "katargeo", and it literally means "to reduce to inactivity" (Vine 1984). This word is also translated "abolished" in 2 Timothy 1:10 referring to Christ who has abolished death and brought life and immortality to light through the Gospel.

The bodily resurrection of Jesus is the result of paralysing death, at the Cross and the one behind it – the Devil. Jesus Christ defeated death because He destroyed the thing that caused it – sin (Rom. 5:12-19). Therefore, Christ is risen from the dead because our sins have been remitted or taken away by the sacrifice of Himself; otherwise, if Christ be not risen, we are yet in our sins (1 Cor. 15:17). When Christ died and was buried, our old nature and sins were destroyed and buried with Him, and when He was raised from the dead, we were also raised a new creation destined to walk in newness of life, no longer bound nor condemned by the old life for it has past away being put to death at the Cross (Rom. 6). He was raised for our justification; no more condemnation (Rom. 8:1).

Jesus Christ was not only raised bodily from the dead, but He ascended to heaven to sit at the right hand of the throne of God, and from that seated position, He continually makes intercession for the saints as their Great High Priest. The apostle states further: "...who is even at the right hand of God, who also maketh intercession for us" (Rom. 8:34).

These clauses tell where Jesus is and what He is doing. Jesus is presently fulfilling His ministry as our High priest in things pertaining to God; the Bible also calls Him our advocate in 2 John 2:1. First of all Jesus being seated at the right hand of God reiterates a profound truth about the work of redemption, contrasting the Levitical sacrificial system and priesthood. The continual offering of animal sacrifices under the Old Covenant could never take away sin to make the worshippers perfect (Heb. 10:1-4). Every year, on the Day of Atonement, animals were sacrificed and their blood taken by the high priest into the Holy of holies to atone for the sins of the people (Heb. 9:7). The high priest had to do this once every year. His work was never finished. But Christ entered once into the heavenly sanctuary with His own blood to appear before God on our behalf (Heb. 9:11-17). And because eternal redemption has been accomplished, there is no need for Him to be sacrificed again for our sins. That is why He now remains seated since all our sins have been purged away (Heb. 1:3). Christ now ever lives to make intercession for us. As the Levitical priest made intercession, with the blood of animals, for the sins of the people, likewise Christ makes intercession, with His own blood, for the sins of the repentant sinners who come to God by Him (Heb. 7:25; Jn. 14:6) and the righteous who stumble and fall (Gal. 6:1; Rom. 8:34; 1 Jn. 2:1). Regarding the last group, as a believer in Christ, if you sin, you will always have an advocate and a helper to go to. Run to Jesus Christ if you sin so that may find mercy and grace to help you in time of need (Heb. 4:16). Christ as our High priest guarantees that your promise of forgiveness is continually secure.

17

The Eternal Security of the Saints

"Who shall separate us from the love of Christ? Shall tribulation, or distress, or persecution, or famine, or nakedness, or peril, or sword? As it is written, For thy sake we are killed all the day long; we are accounted as sheep for the slaughter. Nay, in all these things we are more than conquerors through him that loved us. For I am persuaded, that neither death, nor life, nor angels, nor principalities, nor powers, nor things present, nor things to come, Nor height, nor depth, nor any other creature, shall be able to separate us from the love of God, which is in Christ Jesus our Lord" (Rom. 8:35-39).

Now concerning the eternal security of the believer, the bible sets forth two sides of the same coin as it was also discussed under predestination. Moving too far to either side at the denial or expense of the other will result in an erroneous interpretation of Scripture regarding this subject. The correct biblical view is a balanced approach that embraces equally both sides of this doctrine; the truth is in between. In this chapter, I want to present a balanced approach to this doctrine of eternal security as set forth in Scripture.

There are two aspects of eternal security for the believer presented: the divine responsibility and the human responsibility. With respect to God Himself, He initiated the promise of eternal security for believers and the divine power to preserve and sustain them unto the end. For example, Jude 1:21 and 1 Peter 1:5 read,

"Now unto him that is able to keep thee from falling, and to present you faultless before the presence of his glory with exceeding joy....Who are kept by the power of God through faith unto salvation ready to be revealed in the last time."

Scriptural verses that present human responsibility says,

"Wherefore the rather brethren, give diligence to make your calling and election sure: for if ye do these things, ye shall never fall...But he that shall endure unto the end, the same shall be saved" (2 Peter 1:10; Matt. 24:13).

These scriptural passages among many, present the biblical view that the promise of eternal security must be balanced against the scriptural admonitions and against apostasy according to Hebrews 6 and 10. Eternal security through the power of God includes the human responsibility and freedom of choice to endure with diligence to the end. And these stark warnings are given in such a way that they suggest the possibility of falling away into perdition (Heb. 10:26-29, 35-39).

In the light of eternal security, from the Bible, God preserves those who persevere, and they cannot persevere without God preserving them (1 Thess. 5:23; Eph. 6:18). Here is the true balance of the eternal security of the believer. Furthermore, the scriptural context of Romans 8 and the whole Bible refer to those who have been predestinated and elected unto glorification (Rom. 8:29-30). They will never fall away in to perdition since predestination is the foreordination of all things certain to come to pass, including eternal redemption. Eternal security is a certainty for the elect according to its scriptural context: "Who shall lay anything to the charge of God's elect..." (Rom. 8:33). In Jesus' discourse and teaching on the Mount of Olives, it is stated that unprecedented tribulation, persecution, earthquakes, pestilence, wars and deception would engulf the earth as precursors of His imminent return. But in the midst of Christ's discourse, he said,

"For there shall arise false Christs, and false prophets, and shall shew great signs and wonders, insomuch that, if it were possible, they shall deceive the very elect" (Matt. 24:24).

This verse shows the scale and magnitude of the deception that will take place; it will be so convincing that if it were possible, they would deceive even the elect. But note here; Jesus uses the phrase, "if it were possible", which indicates to me that the elect will not be deceived, but will be preserved by God as they persevere to the end. Even as it was in the days of King Ahab, who plunged the Nation of Israel into the idolatrous practice of Baal worship, influenced by his wife Jezebel, God informed His prophet, Elijah, that he had reserved in Israel seven thousand men who had not bowed their knees to the image of Baal (1 Kgs. 19:18; Rom. 11:4). These passages teach that there is a remnant according to the election of grace (Rom. 11:5). Where there is election, there is a remnant.

The teaching that "once saved, always saved" is foreign to the teachings of the New Testament, and fosters an attitude of complacency and passivity. The promise of eternal security is given to those who will persevere with diligence. Jesus Himself announces His Father's preservation of the elect by saying,

"My sheep hear my voice, and I know them, and they follow me. And I give unto them eternal life, and they shall never perish, neither shall any man pluck them out of my hand. My Father which gave them me, is greater than all, and no man is able to pluck them out of my Father's hand" (Jn. 10:27-29).

Firstly, in the above passage of scripture, Jesus defines eternal security to be eternal life. Secondly, its destiny is that His sheep shall never perish, and thirdly, neither shall any man be able to pluck them out of His hand or His Father's hand. Those whom God has chosen before the foundation of the world have been given to Christ to redeem through His death on the Cross; hence His words, "My Father which gave them me." Jesus stated further, "I know them;" that is, He knows them savingly or knows those who belong to Him (2 Tim. 2:19). In the last days, Jesus will say to those who practice lawlessness, "...I never knew you: depart from me, ye that work iniquity" (Matt. 7:23).

It is also mentioned in the above passage that Christ's sheep will hear His voice and follow Him. In other words, those whom the Lord preserves will hear His voice and follow Him. Hearing His voice and following Him are the means by which He preserves His elect. In the Greek, the terms "hear" and "follow" are in the present tense, which means they are a continuous or repeated action. So Jesus was in actual fact saying that His sheep will continue to hear His voice and continue to follow Him: a description of perseverance. There is a passage of scripture that tells us the condition to possessing eternal life which I also equated to be eternal security:

"He that believeth on the Son hath everlasting life: and he that believeth not the Son shall not see life; but the wrath of God abideth on him" (Jn. 3:36).

The Greek word for "believeth" is also in the present tense: the continuous or repeated action. Therefore, the passage can read like this:

"He that keeps believing on the Son hath eternal life..."

Eternal life is secured to the one who keeps believing. And the next clause of the verse tells us what believing entails,

"...he that believeth not the Son shall not see life; but the wrath of God abideth on him."

The Greek word, in the second clause, for "believeth" is not "pisteuo", but "apeithon", and it means to obey. To believe in the Son also includes to obey Him. He who does not obey the Son shall not see life, but the wrath of God remains upon him as the verse states. Eternal life is promised to those who keep believing and obeying.

Let us now look at the scriptural warnings against apostasy and ensure that we take earnest heed to their warnings. It is in taking heed that our salvation and election are made secure (2 Peter 1:10). Jesus gives us a grave warning in the Parable of the Sower,

"They on the rock are they, which, when they hear, receive the word with joy; and these have no root, which for a while believe, and in time of temptation fall away" (Lk. 8:13).

Jesus gives an example of those who receive the Word with joy and believe at the outset of their Christian life; they are new born babes (1 Peter 2:2). But because they do not have any deep roots in themselves, in time of temptation, they fall away. If once saved, always saved was true, this verse of scripture would not be in the Bible. If people fall away, they are falling away from something. You cannot fall away from something you were never in." It is possible to believe unto saved and falling away. All the apostles who were with Jesus at His time of temptation in the Garden of Gethsemane, predicted that they all would be offended because of Him (Matt. 26:31), but Jesus assured Peter that when he was converted, that is restored back to relationship with Him, he should strengthen the brethren (Lk. 22:31-32). There are those who fall away only to be restored again, and others who fall away into perdition as you will see further in this chapter. As the Apostle John affirms, there is a sin not unto death, and a brother who sins not unto death, we should pray and give life to him. But there is also a sin unto death, and we are commanded not to pray for it (1 Jn. 5:16-17).

In the Olivet discourse of Matthew 24, Jesus predicted that three things would take place to cause many believing Christians to be offended and fall: 1) Christian persecution (v9-10), 2) deception (v11), 3) abundant lawlessness (v12). This lawlessness will cause the love of many to grow cold; but in the midst of these things, Jesus concludes that he who endures to the end the same shall be saved (v13). Resistance to these varieties of temptations will save your soul in the last days. This tells me that what Jesus said about many being offended is a salvation issue.

In the Book of Hebrews, there are two specific warnings given to the Jewish believers against apostatising. One of these warnings is leaving the Christian Faith to return back under the bondage of Mosaic Judaism. They were under great persecution and temptation to abandon the faith of Jesus Christ and revert back to the Law of Moses. And so the Hebrew writer presents his case showing the superiority of Christ over the prophets, angels, Aaron and the Levitical priesthood, the Old Covenant sacrifices and so on. He repeatedly uses the word "better" to present his argument that they would only be returning to something inferior. In his first warning, he states,

"For it is impossible for those who were once enlightened, and have tasted of the heavenly gift, and were made partakers of the Holy Ghost, And have tasted the good word of God, and the powers of the world to come, If they shall fall away, to renew them again unto repentance; seeing they crucify to themselves the Son of God afresh, and put him to an open shame" (Heb. 6:3-6).

This passage of scripture is addressed to believers who have experienced enlightenment, tasted of the heavenly gift, Jesus Christ (1 Peter 2:2-3). They were made partakers of the Holy Spirit: referring to the baptism in the Holy Spirit, and have tasted the good Word of God (1 Peter 1:23), and the powers of the age to come. These refer to believers who have experienced salvation. The passage is saying that it is impossible for those who have fallen away, to renew these experiences unto repentance, seeing they have crucified to themselves the Son of God afresh and have put Him to an open shame. That means to have nothing more to do with Christ and treat Him with open contempt and despicable disregard – a wilful act of sin.

The second scriptural warning confirms the first as being an act of wilful sin after partaking of the knowledge of salvation, also called being "enlightened." It reads,

"For if we sin wilfully after that we have received the knowledge of the truth, there remaineth no more sacrifice for sin, But a certain fearful looking for of judgment and fiery indignation, which shall devour the adversaries. He that despised Moses' law died without mercy under two or three witnesses: Of how much sorer punishment, suppose ye, shall he be thought worthy, who hath trodden under foot the Son of God, and hath counted the blood of the covenant, wherewith he was sanctified, an unholy thing, and hath done despite unto the Spirit of grace?" (Heb. 10:26-29)

Here are some key points, from the above passage, to consider: the Hebrew writer warns of apostatising by sinning wilfully after having received the knowledge of the truth. The term "knowledge" here is alluding to an experiential, intimate, relational knowledge of the truth; a relationship between the knower and the object of the knowledge, and its Greek designation is "epignosis"; full and exact knowledge. It refers to being a partaker of the truth.

The consequence of wilful sin is that there remaineth no more sacrifice for sins. The Hebrew writer, having indepth knowledge of the Mosaic Law, relates comparatively to the fact that under the Levitical sacrificial system, there was no sacrificial provision made for wilful and presumptuous sins, only sins of ignorance (see Lev. 4:1-2, 13, 22, 27). In like manner, the sacrifice of the Son of God was made to expiate sins of ignorance, not wilful sins. Hence, the statement is made, "...there remaineth no more sacrifice for sins." That is why when Jesus was on the cross, He said "Father forgive them; for they know not what they do" (Lk. 23:34). When Peter spoke to His Jewish audience, he announced to them that they were guilty of killing the Prince of life, and called them to repentance because they had done it in ignorance (Acts 3:13-15, 17, 19; Num. 15:24-29, 30-36). The Apostle Paul stated in his epistle that he was a blasphemer and persecutor of the church but obtained mercy and forgiveness because he did it in ignorance (1 Tim. 1:13).

Again, he who despised Moses' Law died without mercy under two or three witnesses. While no sacrificial provision was made under the Old Covenant for the wilful despising of Moses' Law, the penalty was death by two or three witnesses (Deut. 13:1-15; 17:2-7). However, King David was an exception. He received mercy by divine intervention when he committed adultery and murder which were punishable by death, but even then, there was no sacrifice that he could offer. Although God forgave him, he was chastised severely (2 Sam. 12; Ps. 51).

The object of this wilful apostasy is threefold: firstly, those who commit this sin have trodden under foot the Son of God – treating a Divine Person with wilful contempt, having full knowledge of what they have done. They would not even be concerned about whether they have committed the unpardonable sin or not. Their hearts have become hardened. Furthermore, they count the blood of the Covenant, with which they were sanctified, an unholy thing. They treat it as common and without value by rejecting its saving power, even after they were saved and sanctified by it (2 Thess. 2:13; 1 Peter 1:2. And lastly, to commit such a sin is to treat with insult the pleadings and promptings of the Spirit of grace. The Greek rendering for "despite" is "enubrizo", meaning to insult. With these in mind, the Hebrew writer ensures a more severe punishment than the despisers of Moses' Law. The bible informs that how shall we escape if we neglect such a great salvation (Heb. 2:3).

The Apostle Peter warns about those who escaped the pollutions of the world through the knowledge of Jesus Christ, who become entangled again in bondage; their latter end being worse than their beginning. For it had been better for them not to have known the way of righteousness, than to know and turn from it (2 Peter 3:20-22).

Eternal security of the believer is the embracing of the promise of eternal life, taking heed to the warnings against apostasy and persevering to the end by the power of the Holy Spirit. And with this balance in mind, nothing can separate us from the love of God in Christ Jesus. There were those who have already gone on before us, who endured to the end and are now awaiting us. I leave with you these words of exhortation:

"keep yourselves in the love of God...We know that whosoever is born of God sinneth not; but he that is begotten of God keepeth himself, and that wicked one toucheth him not" (Jude 1:21a, 1 Jn. 5:18).

Bibliography

Vine, W. E. (1984) "An Expository Dictionary of New Testament Words," Chicago: Moody Press

Hodge, A. A. (1983) "Outlines of Theology," Pennsylvania: The Banner of Truth Trust

www.ingramcontent.com/pod-product-compliance
Lightning Source LLC
Chambersburg PA
CBHW021128300426
44113CB00006B/342